Conversation Peace

The Power of Transformed Speech

Mary A. Kassian

LifeWay Press®
Nashville, Tennessee

ISBN 9780633007614
Item 001114551

Dewey Decimal Classification Number: 302.2
Subject Heading: GOSSIP \ CONVERSATION

Unless otherwise noted, Scripture quotations are from the Holy Bible, New International
Version, copyright © 1973, 1978, 1984 by International Bible Society. Scripture quotations
marked KJV are from the King James Version.

To order additional copies of this resource: Write LifeWay Church Resources Customer Service;
One LifeWay Plaza; Nashville, TN 37234-0113; fax order to (615) 251-5933;
phone (800) 458-2772; order online at *www.lifeway.com*;
or visit the LifeWay Christian Store serving you.

Printed in the United States of America

Leadership and Adult Publishing
LifeWay Church Resources
One LifeWay Plaza
Nashville, Tennessee 37234-0175

Contents

About Mary 4
About This Study 5

Week 1 Element:
The Power of Navigation 6

Week 2 Element:
The Power of Cause and Effect .28

Week 3 Element:
The Power of Exchange 50

Week 4 Element:
The Power of the Open Gate 72

Week 5 Element:
The Power of Construction 94

Week 6 Element:
The Power of Instruction 116

Week 7 Element:
The Power of Return 138

Leader Guide 140
Christian Growth Study Plan 146
Breath Freshener Cards 147

About Mary

Mary Kassian leads an organization called Alabaster Flask Ministries that challenges young women to love God extravagantly and to joyfully embrace His design for them. She speaks and teaches classes and workshops to women at seminaries and churches across North America.

Mary is the author of several books, including *In My Father's House: Women Relating to God as Father* (LifeWay Press), Bible studies, poems, and worship liturgies. She is a doctoral student in systematic theology at the University of South Africa.

Mary A. Kassian

At home in Sherwood Park, Alberta, Canada, she watches lots of sports! Three teenage sons play ice hockey, and her husband, Brent, is chaplain for a professional football team. The Kassians enjoy biking, hiking, snorkeling, music, board games, mountains, campfires, and their family's black lab, General Beau.

Mary thanks all the women in her Calvary Baptist Church small group who helped birth this study: Sue, Anne, Christine, Lillian, Sharon, Kim, Denise, Kelly, and Dayna.

Mary says, "At their deepest root, communication problems are spiritual problems. As such, they require spiritual solutions, and for that, we must turn to God. This study presents seven powerful speech-transforming elements that are based on the Bible. For the final word on how to transform our words, the Bible is our book! It sets a high standard for speech and also for thoughts and attitudes. But even more important, it reveals the *secret* for how to reach that standard—God's power. Not some magical formula or phrase. Not the *right* technique or combination of words.

"That's not to say that practical techniques are of no use. We'll be learning how to listen, use body language, resolve conflict, express ourselves clearly, say I'm sorry, resist manipulation, set a positive communication climate and more! This workbook is chock full of practical advice.

"But at heart, this study is about God changing our hearts. He has given us His Word to transform and revolutionize our words and lead us into *Conversation Peace*. Join me as we accept His exciting offer!"

About This Study

Do you want to experience the power of transformed speech? *Conversation Peace* is an interactive Bible study that includes seven videos for viewing and discussion in small groups. The member workbook provides six weeks of daily, individual study materials for use between sessions. Here's what you'll get:

Daily Lessons

The daily lessons, to be completed on your own, should take no more than 20 minutes. Each week's lessons will help you harness the power of one speech-transforming element: the power of navigation, the power of cause and effect, the power of exchange, the power of the open gate, the power of construction, the power of instruction, and the power of return.

Weekly Talk Show

At the beginning of each week, participants gather to participate in small-group discussions (talk), and to watch a video presentation by Mary Kassian (show). A Talk Show guide is included on the second page of each week's lessons. A leader guide is provided on pages 140-145.

Tongue Tonic

[*ton•ic*] ton'ik, [Gr. *tonikos*] a solution that maintains, increases, or restores the health of the system or organ. The Tongue Tonics explored in this study contain practical concepts and skills to help increase or restore the health of your speech. Whenever you see the symbol, stop and take a dose.

Word from the Word

Each Word from the Word defines, explains, and helps you understand how to apply certain words from the Bible. God's Words will stimulate you to think about the way you use words. Study each Word from the Word and watch your vocabulary grow strong and healthy!

Quips and Quotes

A lot of people have said good things about how to use our mouths. Quips and quotes contain gems of speech–wisdom from noted philosophers and historical and religious figures. Profound, witty, and wise, Quips and Quotes are sure to inspire and challenge you.

Breath Freshener

Freshen your breath by memorizing the Scripture verse for the week. Cut-out cards are included on page 147 so you can tuck the Breath Fresheners into your purse or pocket.

The Power of Navigation

Our tongues determine the direction of our lives.

The Bible compares the tongue to a rudder of a ship and to a bit in the mouth of a horse. Though relatively small, all three of these–the rudder, the bit, and the tongue–have tremendous power. A rudder turns a ship, a bit turns a horse, and our tongues turn our lives in the direction we will go. Your tongue can take you into calm or troubled waters or make or break your relationships. This week harness the power of navigation to turn your tongue in the right direction.

Where do you want to go today? God wants to take you to all sorts of exciting and fascinating places. In this week's Talk Show you will discover that where you go today depends on what you say today.

Day 1: Understanding the Role of the Rudder
   The tongue is our principal steering mechanism.
Day 2: Launching a Warship or Merchant Ship
   The tongue can be used as a weapon or tool.
Day 3: Setting Out on Course
   The chart maps the way of wisdom.
Day 4: Maneuvering the Vessel
   Maritime rules provide for a safe voyage.
Day 5: Taking Our Bearings
   Tools help determine our position.

This Week's Tongue Tonics:
   • Three Parts of a Message
   • Sending a Message
   • The Communication Loop
   • Eight Potential Problems in Communication

"For 'whoever would love life and see good days must keep his tongue from evil and his lips from deceitful speech. He must turn from evil and do good; he must seek peace and pursue it'" (1 Pet. 3:10-11).

Cut out the Scripture card on page 147 as a reminder this week.

The Power of Navigation: Where do you want to go today?

James 3:1-6

This Talk Show guide will help you follow the video for Session One.

The tongue has the power of life or _____. Tongues navigate our ships. James compares our tongues to a rudder and a bit.

1. The tongue navigates.

a. Words _____ our world (see Heb. 11:3).
A supporting structure or skeleton defines the shape and boundary for all that it contains.

b. Words _____ (see Rom. 10:9-10).
Your speech is a confession that either aligns you with God's view of reality or with someone else's.

c. Words have _____ consequences (see Matt. 18:18).
They can "bind" and "loose."

d. Words affect our _____ (see Matt. 12:36-37).

Your _____ will either acquit or condemn you.

2. Charts and tools are provided.

a. The _____ charts the course (see Jas. 1:25).
We will be on course if we follow the right chart.

b. _____ take our bearings (see John 16:8-16).
Some of these are our consciences, feedback from family and friends, and the gift of the Holy Spirit.

3. Order at the helm is required.

a. Accept _____ (see Jas. 1:26; 3:7-8).

b. Get help (see Ps. 18:30-32).
To be totally responsible yet totally _____ is the paradox of the disciple of Christ and the paradox of successful navigation.

Where you go today depends on what you say today.

Day One
Understanding the Role of the Rudder
The tongue is our principal steering mechanism.

"So also the tongue is a small thing, but what enormous damage it can do. A great forest can be set on fire by one tiny spark. And the tongue is a flame of fire. It is full of wickedness, and poisons every part of the body ... and can turn our whole lives into a blazing flame of destruction and disaster."
James 3:5-6,
The Living
Bible

This summer my youngest son will make his maiden voyage as captain of the fishing boat. This right of passage happens at about the 12th year of every Kassian's life. As instructed, the new captain will display his skill by taking five or six passes close to the shoreline bordering the cabin. Dad, Mom, Grandma, Grandpa, aunts, uncles, siblings, and any other spectators in the vicinity will shout and cheer. Camcorders will whir, and shutters will snap.

The highlight of the demonstration occurs when the captain navigates the boat around in a broad circle and pulls back in along the pier. Victoriously, he'll turn off the motor, dock the boat, and run ashore to receive his accolades. Passing this test earns him the right to take the small boat out to go fishing in front of the cabin.

In the Bible, the apostle James compares our tongues to a ship's rudder. Steering a boat is based on a relatively simple concept. It operates on the principle of unequal water pressures. When a rudder is turned so that one side is more exposed to the force of the water, the stern (back) of the boat will rotate toward the side of the rudder where the water pressure is less.

In small craft the rudder is connected to a handle called a tiller and turned manually. In larger vessels, it is turned by hydraulic, steam, or electrical machinery. In all cases, the rudder is relatively small but is responsible for setting the direction of the whole vessel.

This week we'll study the first element of transformed speech–the Power of Navigation. We'll learn that, just like a rudder, our tongues turn our lives in the direction we will go.

Read James 3:2-6. Note the illustrations James uses for the tongue in verses 3 and 4: a bit in the mouth of a horse and a rudder of a ship. For each of these, record in the chart below what might happen if the object were used incorrectly and what would happen if used correctly.

Object	Used Incorrectly	Used Correctly
Bit in horse's mouth		
Rudder of a ship		

In what way do these illustrations reflect the situation with our tongues?

_____

James wants us to realize that our tongues are our principal steering mechanism. What we talk is where we'll walk. If we use our tongues for good, we will head in the right direction. If we use our tongues for evil, we will steer our ship towards destruction.

The Tongue Is a Spark of Fire

In James 3:6, James compares the tongue to a spark of fire that burns down an entire forest. According to James, the tongue sets the whole course of a person's life on fire. In the *Revised Standard Version* of the Bible, the phrase is translated as "the wheel of nature." The Greek word is *trochos*, which means "genesis" or beginning. By using this word, James implied that the tongue is the hub– the beginning–of "the whole round of human life and activity."[1]

On the wheel, write the first names of some of your family members, friends, coworkers, or neighbors. Your tongue affects all the relationships you recorded. It is the hub that influences the whole circle of your life.

If the hub of a wheel is on fire, the fire can quickly burn in all directions down the spokes to the rim of the wheel. From the burning hub, the whole wheel can be engulfed in flames. James' point is that our tongues play a central, "hub-like" role in our lives. He wants us to recognize that a small spark of evil on our tongue has the capacity to destroy our relationships and even our whole lives.

Sparks remind me of what happened to my older brother, Gordon, who was trying to light a coal barbeque. He tried repeatedly, but it wouldn't light. As a final resort, he decided to use gasoline. He did not know a small spark had, in fact, taken hold in the coals. The spark was too small to see. It didn't let off any noticeable smoke or heat. But when Gordon poured gasoline on the coals, the whole barbeque exploded. His burns, to more than 70 percent of his body, were life-threatening. Thankfully, by the grace of God he recovered. But he had to endure excruciating pain and months of rehabilitation.

Not many of you have experienced the pain of badly burned flesh, but many of you have experienced the pain of badly burned relationships. Life has poured gasoline on your coals. The sparks hidden in your tongue and in the tongues of your loved ones have exploded into a destructive fire. The pain–and the rehabilitation–will be lengthy.

Steer in the Right Direction

How we choose to use our tongues–for good or for evil–affects our whole life. It affects the type of person we become and the type experiences we will have.

Read Proverbs 12:5-8,13-22. In the appropriate column, summarize the characteristics and life experiences of those who use their tongues for evil (wickedness) and those who use their tongues for good (righteousness).

Use their tongues for evil	Use their tongues for good

Our Breath Freshener for the week (see p. 6) sums up the two benefits of controlling our tongues. What are they?

Benefit 1:

_____

Benefit 2:

_____

We have been reminded of the importance of our tongues. Like a rudder, they set the direction for our lives. Using our tongues in the right way will bring us blessing. We will love life and see good days.

How do we begin to steer our vessels in the right direction? Our Breath Freshener gives us a clue: "turn from evil and do good, seek peace and pursue it." To *pursue* means *to chase after.* A pursuit requires time, energy, and commitment. Turning–changing–our words from evil to good also requires time, energy, and commitment. Above all, it requires study to find out what God has to say about how to use our mouths and to ask Him to help us use them in the right way. Why don't you close today's lesson by talking to God? Ask Him to help you "turn from evil and do good, seek peace and pursue it."

A word is dead when it is said, some say. I say it just begins to live that day.
—Emily Dickinson

Today's Tongue Tonic will explain the three parts of a message.

Three Parts of a Message

When we interact with others, the messages we send are made up of three parts: (1) verbal–the words we speak, (2) vocal–the tone of our voice, and (3) visual–our body language. How much weight do you think each part contributes to the overall message? Write your guess beside each word.

VERBAL: We express our thoughts with words. Words can be precise or imprecise, weighted (always, never, ever, only, all, really, just), accusing ("You are…"), intense or mild (furious, annoyed), vague ("sort of"), pleading or demanding. Though words are invaluable in articulating our thoughts and ideas, research indicates that in personal interaction, words only contribute seven percent to the overall message.[2]

VOCAL: More important than words we speak is the tone of voice we use. Our voices are incredibly versatile. We can emphasize certain words; clip, force, or soften words; speak in a lilting, sing-songy, mimicking, or sneering tone; speak rapidly or slowly; over- or under-articulate, raise or lower the volume; and/or change the pitch. The possibilities are endless. Tone of voice contributes 38 percent to the overall message.

VISUAL: Body language is the final and most important part of interpersonal interaction. Again, the possibilities are endless. Consider how the following visual cues affect the message: roll eyes, shake or tilt head, shrug shoulders, frown, purse lips, squint, raise eyebrows, furrow brow, cross arms, glare, sneer, lack of eye contact, rapid blink, glance side to side, point finger, exaggerate arm/hand gestures, tap fingers. Visual cues contribute 55 percent to the overall message.

All three parts of a message must align and be consistent in order for the message to be believed. For example, if you say you accept someone, but you say it with a tense voice and crossed arms, chances are they won't believe you. For the message to be clear, all three parts must "say" the same thing.

Day Two
Launching a Warship or Merchant Ship
The tongue can be used as a weapon or tool.

"A woman of noble character is like the merchant ships."
Proverbs 31:14

When it comes to preparing meals, I'm the practical type. "Fast" and "simple" are the two characteristics of all my recipes. With a house full of teenage boys, "voluminous" and "cheap" have recently been added to my list of menu requirements. On the other hand, my husband Brent enjoys spending a Saturday or Sunday afternoon chopping and mixing exotic ingredients in order to sauté, baste, braise, or broil the latest dish featured on his favorite cooking show. (Bam!–throw in some spices–kick it up a notch!)

Often Brent complains about the condition of our kitchen knives. The bargain-store set we received as a wedding gift 18 years ago just weren't cutting it (pardon the pun). How could he achieve culinary excellence when his scallions and shallots were getting mulched instead of thinly sliced? His frustration reached such a point that one day I found all my knives, save one, in the garbage can. (Being the practical type, I rescued them.)

For our anniversary, I will give Brent a set of heavy-duty, professional chef knives. They lie in wait on black velvet in a glass- and aluminum-enclosed case. Just a few moments ago, I opened the case and lightly brushed my thumb against the edge of the largest knife.

It's very sharp. An edge like that is certain to cut.

A sharp knife is an essential tool for cooking, but a sharp knife can also be used as a weapon. The same edge can create or kill, depending on how it is used. The Hebrew word *mouth (peh)* is often translated *edge*. Like a knife, the tongue has a sharp, powerful edge that can either create or destroy. It functions as a helpful tool or a destructive weapon—depending on its use.

Read Psalm 57:4. Put your creative talents to use. Using the description provided in this passage, draw in the box a picture of what David's enemies looked like.

David's enemies probably carried weapons in their hands, but these weapons concerned him the least. The ones with potential to cut him most deeply were the sharp edges of his enemies' tongues.

According to Psalm 64:3-4, what did David's enemies do with their tongues?

_____

_____

_____

A wound inflicted by the tongue bleeds the spirit more severely than a wound inflicted by the sword bleeds the flesh. Have you ever felt wounded by the sharp edge of someone's tongue? Have you ever felt ambushed? Attacked? Cut to pieces? I have. People have hurt me deeply with their words. But it's sobering for me to realize that my mouth carries the same edge as theirs. It has the same destructive potential.

A blow with a word strikes deeper than a blow with a sword.
—Robert Burton

Draw a line to connect the verses with the words describing the destructive power of the tongue:

Psalm 140:3   lash or whip
Proverbs 16:27   scorching fire
Proverbs 18:7   snare
Job 5:21   deadly arrow
Jeremiah 9:8   poison of vipers

God wants us to be aware of the potential of our tongues—potential for evil and for good. According to Proverbs 12:18, we use our tongues for evil when we speak recklessly. "Reckless words pierce like a sword." The same verse outlines what happens when we use our tongues wisely—as a tool.

"Reckless words pierce like a sword, but the tongue of the wise brings healing."
Proverbs 12:18

What happens when we use our tongues wisely? (Check one.)
❏ The sword chops us up.
❏ We get a mouth full of dirt.
❏ We dig our enemy's grave.
❏ Our words bring healing.

In the ancient world, swords were the most common weapons of war. The Bible tells us that during war, the Hebrews would make swords from their plowshares (see Joel 3:10). A plowshare is the cutting edge of a plow—the agricultural tool that cuts furrows in the soil and prepares the ground for planting. When peace returned, the Hebrews hammered the swords back into plows (see Isa. 2:4; Mic. 4:3). The edge that killed the enemy in war was the same edge that helped provide food in peace. The sharp edge had two functions.

> A sharp tongue is the only edge tool that grows sharper with constant use.
> —Washington Irving

Likewise, our tongues can operate in one of two ways: we can declare war and use it to pierce, wound, and kill, or we can use it as an instrument of peace—plowing the soil of our relationships to make them rich and fruitful.

Consider the words that came out of your mouth in the past few days. Were there times that you used your mouth as a sword?
❑ Yes ❑ No

Can you think of instances when you used the edge of your tongue in a positive way, to open up the soil of your relationships—helping them become rich and fruitful? ❑ Yes ❑ No

Are you satisfied with the harvest you are reaping, consistently using your mouth as a tool to cultivate a bountiful harvest?
❑ Yes, I consistently use my mouth as a tool to positively cultivate all my relationships.
❑ I am inconsistent. Sometimes I use my mouth as a tool to cultivate, and sometimes I use it as a weapon to harm.
❑ No, I often use my mouth as a weapon and have difficulty using it as a tool to cultivate my relationships.

Launch the Right Kind of Ship

If you choose to use your tongue as a sword, your relationships will experience perpetual calamity. On the other hand, if you choose to put your sword into its sheath (a mark of peace and friendship), pound it into a plow, and begin to till the soil of your relationships, you will reap rich rewards (see Prov. 12:14).

The word *plow* (Latin—*aratio)* literally means, "to open up the soil." It is closely related to the anglo-saxon *ar* from which we derive the English word *oar*—a rudder that plows the sea. As we learned yesterday, the tongue is our principal steering mechanism. It is the rudder that sets the direction of our vessel. Understanding the role of the rudder is the first part of harnessing the power of navigation. Launching the right kind of ship is the second.

In ancient Rome, two types of ships sailed the seas: warships and merchant ships. The merchant ships were large, high-sided vessels with two or three masts that flew square sails. Their primary purpose was to transport grain from Egypt to Italy to feed the expanding Roman population.

The warships were visibly different. They carried dozens of fighting men and were equipped with catapults and ramming rods. Instead of being propelled by wind-billowed sails, the warships were propelled by banks of oarsmen: prisoners and slaves chained under the ship's deck. Compared to the merchant ships, warships were lighter, longer, and more slender—designed for rapid attack and evasive maneuvers.

Which ship will you launch? Will you use your tongue as a sword on a warship or use it as a plow to fill the hull of a merchant ship with nourishing grain? If you've been using your tongue as a weapon, why don't you ask God to help you pound that sword into a plow?

Today's Tongue Tonic outlines potential communication problems.

Sending a Message

When a person sends a message, it is encoded—packaged—through his or her personality, feelings, attitudes, assumptions, habits, past experiences, and current environment. A person who is stressed will encode a message differently than someone who is relaxed. A passive person will encode a message differently than an aggressive one. Someone who values frankness will encode a message differently than one who values tact.

An encoded message is presented behaviorally—through words, tone of voice, and body language. The receiver observes this behavior and decodes the message based on his or her own personality, feelings, attitudes, assumptions, habits, past experiences, and current environment. That is why two people listening to the same speaker can receive two entirely different messages.

The Communication Loop

The process of sending and receiving messages is normally not a one-way street. In person-to-person communication, each individual sends and receives messages simultaneously. As I am talking, I am also observing and decoding your response. As you are observing and decoding my behavior, you are encoding and sending messages with your behavior. Our interaction forms a communication loop.

Eight Potential Problems in Communication

In each communication loop, there are eight potential problems. Miscommunication can occur when either person has difficulty encoding his or her own message or decoding the other person's message. It can also occur when either person's behavior does not match the intended encoding, or when either person is faulty in his or her observation of the other person's behavior. So in an interaction where each person speaks only one sentence, there are 16 ways in which miscommunication can occur!

The Eight Potential Problems

1. Person A's encoding
2. Person A's decoding
3. Person A's observation
4. Person A's behavior
5. Person B's decoding
6. Person B's encoding
7. Person B's behavior
8. Person B's observation

Day Three

Setting Out on Course
The chart maps the way of wisdom.

"How much better to get wisdom than gold, to choose understanding rather than silver! The highway of the upright avoids evil; he who guards his way guards his life."
Proverbs 16:16-17

Drive past Walmart until you get to the gas station. Turn left. Drive for about five minutes. When the road curves to the right, look for a green mailbox. Our house is the one with the big black dog in front.

Have you ever tried to follow poor directions? Chances are good that somewhere along the way, we will miss a turn and never get back on course. I remember missing a wedding shower when a friend gave me directions that omitted one important turn. After driving around in circles for an hour-and-a-half, I finally gave up and returned home.

If we want to get where we're going, good directions are crucial. As we learned in this week's video, we are not left on our own to navigate our way through the waters of life. The Bible charts a course for us. The instructions are clear; the directions are good. In the Book of Proverbs, the Bible's route is identified as the "way of wisdom."

How Do We Know We Are on Course?

Proverbs 4:5-27 records what a wise father once told his son about setting out on the right course.

Read this passage in your Bible. The words *straight*, *light*, *level*, and *firm* describe the characteristics of the way of wisdom. The path of foolishness is just the opposite: crooked, dark, uneven, and treacherous.

"My son, if your heart is wise, then my heart will be glad; my inmost being will rejoice when your lips speak what is right."
Proverbs 23:15-16

Read Proverbs 23:15-16. Check the answer that states how the way of wisdom would affect the son's speech:
❏ He would become a politician.
❏ He would speak what is right.
❏ He would stop stuttering.

The father would be able to tell if his son were following the way of wisdom by observing the way the son used his mouth. Those who walk in wisdom avoid perverse, corrupt speech. The son's speech would be the primary indicator as to whether or not he was on course. It's the same way with us. Our mouths indicate whether or not we are on course. If we are steering our vessels the right way, our lips will speak what is right.

The map below illustrates some destinations we could choose for our tongues. Identify which *islands* correspond to the verses listed in the column to the right. Write the name(s) of the islands under the matching verses.

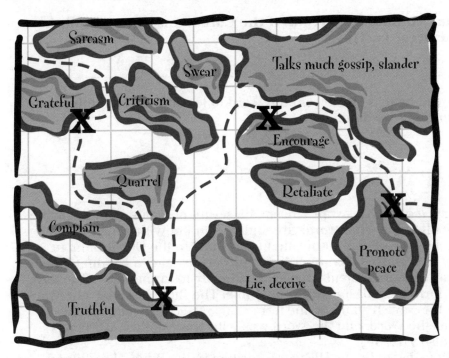

Proverbs 3:17

Proverbs 14:5

Proverbs 20:19

Ephesians 5:4

Philippians 2:14

First Thessalonians 5:11

The way of wisdom is marked with an X. Mark a line on the map indicating the course you are currently following.

How Do We Find Wisdom?

Where can we go to find wisdom? A quick search on the Internet presents all sorts of possibilities—Buddhism, Witch Wisdom, Islam, Kabbalah, Dalai Lama, Metaphysics, ancient philosophers, the Ascended Master's Network, Lotus Gardens—the list goes on and on.

The advice is often contradictory. In search of wisdom I could shave my head, grow my hair long, wear weird clothes, chant, hum, remain silent, light candles, burn incense, fast, feast, join a commune, meditate in solitude, or become a disciple of numerous spiritual leaders and guides. With all these options, how can we find a source of wisdom that's reliable?

> Wisdom is oftentimes nearer when we stoop than when we soar.
> —William Wordsworth

The Bible says that there are two types of wisdom: "the wisdom that comes from heaven," and a counterfeit wisdom that is "earthly" and "unspiritual" (Jas. 3:13-17).

According to Colossians 2:2-4, where are all the treasures of true spiritual wisdom and knowledge hidden?

_____

What would be the result if the Colossians did not find these treasures? (v. 4)

_____

Read today's Word from the Word to learn more about this source of spiritual wisdom.

[word] A SPECIAL MESSAGE

The dictionary defines _word_ in this way: "the smallest unit of meaningful linguistic communication." We all know what words are. But do you know that the Bible refers to _the Word_ as a special type of communication from God? In the Old Testament, the term _the Word of God_ is used 394 times to identify a message—a commandment, prophesy, warning, or encouragement—God spoke directly to humankind. The term includes the written form of God's message—the Bible. The Bible is called "the Word of God" (Ps. 119). In the New Testament, the term is also used as a name for Jesus: "In the beginning was the Word, and the Word was with God, and the Word was God" (John 1:1, see also vv. 2-18).

God interacts with us by giving us His words written in the Bible. His ultimate act of communication comes through the gift of His Son. Jesus— the Word, the Son of God—"became flesh and made his dwelling among us. We have seen his glory, the glory of the One and Only, who came from the Father, full of grace and truth" (John 1:14). You see, God's Word is His communication to you. Are you listening to His special message?

"He who trusts in himself is a fool, but he who walks in wisdom is kept safe."
Proverbs 28:26

In 312 A.D., Roman Emperor Constantine the Great was preparing to battle Emperor Maxentius, who had gathered a great number of legions in defiance of Constantine's leadership. Prior to the battle, Constantine saw a powerful vision in the sky: a _Chi-Rho_ symbol in which were emblazoned the words: "In this sign you will conquer."

The _Chi-Rho_ is a Christian symbol representing Jesus Christ, with the _chi_ and _rho_ being the first two Greek letters of Christ's name. Constantine placed this sign on his standards and had it painted on his shields. He won the day with a decisive victory against Maxentius, converted to Christianity, and soon became the sole emperor of the Roman Empire, ending years of political instability. Constantine is known for granting religious freedom and stopping the persecution of Christians with the Edict of Milan, and for his prominent role at the Council of Nicaea, which countered false beliefs about the Holy Trinity.

The coins used during Constantine's time depict the emperor standing in a ship (representing the empire), holding a banner bearing the *Chi-Rho* symbol. At the rear of the ship, the allegorical female figure "Victory" holds the rudder. The symbolic meaning is plain: with the emperor ruling under the banner of Christ, the empire would be guided in victory along the right path.

As you stand under the banner of Christ, your ship will be guided in victory along the way of wisdom. As you set out on course, why don't you resolve to look to Christ, the Source of all wisdom and understanding? The apostle James said, "If any of you lacks wisdom, he should ask God, who gives generously to all without finding fault, and it will be given to him" (Jas. 1:5).

Today's Tongue Tonic addresses the various goals of communication. Why do you talk?

Prime Objective

Why talk? Check all those that apply:

- ❑ to demonstrate my superior wit and intelligence
- ❑ to get my way
- ❑ to vent
- ❑ to pass on information
- ❑ to qualify for the Ms. Congeniality award
- ❑ to conform to social expectations
- ❑ to help the plants grow
- ❑ to fill air space

Communication goals vary from conversation to conversation. In a business relationship, the goal may be to transmit instructions or directives. At a social gathering, the goal may be to break an awkward silence or to make someone feel welcome. Goals in communication vary, but the prime objective in communication does not.

When **receiving** a message, the prime objective is to understand the message. When **sending** a message, the prime objective is to convey the message clearly.

Some people are afraid to seek understanding because they feel that doing so will signify agreement. Conversely, some people do not feel their messages have been heard until the listener consents to the message. Effective communicators do not make this false association. In every interaction, they make understanding and clarity—not agreement or consent—their prime objective.

Day Four

Maneuvering the Vessel
Maritime rules provide for a safe voyage

The first time I snorkeled in the ocean, I felt exhilarated–unlike anything I had ever experienced! A whole new world: amber, indigo, and emerald shapes on an iridescent crystal canvas. The sea life was astonishing in shape and variety–Sea Turtles, Raccoon Fish, Long-nosed Butterfly Fish, Gilded Triggerfish, Fantail, Needlefish, Moorish Idol, Little Bitty Yellow Tang–each discovery a new delight. When I released a handful of frozen peas into the water, a shimmering curtain of finned creatures flittered around me, bumping and nudging to get at the small, green, floating orbs. The coral reef teemed with life!

Sadly, the ocean is also a place of death. The vulnerable are under constant threat. Predators kill creatures smaller and weaker than themselves. Swimmers drown. The swell of a hurricane demolishes homes. Storms and squalls capsize mighty vessels or smash them on rocks like toys. Many have suffered, and many have died in the arms of the water's cruel fury.

The Power of Our Tongues

According to Proverbs 18:21, how are our tongues like the ocean?

_____

When we bless others with our words, it is as though we figuratively breathe life into them. When we curse or criticize, it is as though we figuratively cripple and kill them. But the Bible teaches that the power of our tongues is more than just figurative.

Read Matthew 12:36-37. When we stand before God, on what basis will He evaluate us? (Check one.)
- ❏ our good intentions
- ❏ our church attendance
- ❏ our words and speech
- ❏ our charitable giving

All those who come in contact with the ocean should have a healthy respect for its life-and-death power. All of us ought to have a healthy respect for the life-and-death power of the tongue. Failing to respect the tongue's power can lead to a disaster of gigantic proportions.

"In times like the present, men should utter nothing for which they would not willingly be responsible through time and eternity."
—Abraham Lincoln

Regulating the Tongue

A portion of this week's video was filmed on the helm of a British Columbia ferry during its crossing from Vancouver to Swartz Bay, the ferry terminal just outside of Victoria. Three days before our film crew boarded that ferry, it had collided with a small yacht, killing one man and critically injuring a woman.

The captain of the ferry had spotted the yacht, repeatedly sounded the horn, and attempted to make radio contact. He followed all the applicable maritime procedures. But for whatever reason, the captain of the yacht didn't. The consequences of his neglect were fatal.

Before taking their vessels to sea, captains must be well-versed in standard maritime rules and procedures. Governing agencies have formulated maritime rules so that each boater can have a safe, enjoyable voyage. In the same way, God has provided rules and procedures for us which are intended to make life's voyage safe and enjoyable. God's rules are recorded in the Bible. They are known by various names such as precepts, statutes, words, ordinances, laws, commands, or ways.

> The strength of a man consists in finding out the way God is going, and going that way.
> —Henry Ward Beecher

Read what David, the shepherd who became a king, had to say about God's regulations in Psalm 19:7-11:

> The law of the Lord is perfect, reviving the soul. The statutes of the Lord are trustworthy, making wise the simple. The precepts of the Lord are right, giving joy to the heart. The commands of the Lord are radiant, giving light to the eyes. The fear [respect] of the Lord is pure, enduring forever. The ordinances of the Lord are sure and altogether righteous. They are more precious than gold, than much pure gold; they are sweeter than honey, than honey from the comb. By them is your servant warned; in keeping them there is great reward.

Use the verses above to complete the following activities:

1. Circle all the adjectives David used to describe God's regulations. (The first adjective is *perfect*.)

2. List some benefits of following His regulations.

_____ _____

_____ _____

_____ _____

The following verses outline additional benefits of respecting God and following His commands. Write the reference of each verse below the symbol with which it corresponds.

Psalm 69:1   Psalm 107:30   Psalm 119:105   Hebrews 6:19

_____   _____   _____   _____

Wise captains realize that regulations are for their benefit—not to unduly restrict them. Therefore, they esteem and appreciate the rules and are careful to follow them. In the same way, God's standard is not meant to restrict us. James identifies it as "the perfect law that gives freedom" (Jas. 1:25). Just as following maritime rules gives sailors the freedom to enjoy the sea, so following God's rules gives us the freedom to enjoy our lives. If we are wise, we will be careful to esteem, appreciate, and follow His ways.

Read today's Word from the Word to learn more about the proper way to communicate.

[co.mú.ni.ca.te] THE EMPHASIS BELONGS ON "U"

The Greek word for *communicate* is *koinⁿnia,* which means "to share, partake, have fellowship with, to join together." It is used in Hebrews 13:15-16: "Through Jesus, therefore, let us continually offer to God a sacrifice of praise—the fruit of lips that confess his name. And do not forget to do good and to share [communicate] with others, for with such sacrifices God is pleased." According to this verse, I "share" when I give to others. It is a "sacrifice" because the focus is not on myself but on the other person. In true communication, I am more interested in understanding than being understood, in listening than being listened to, and in giving than getting. I am less interested in me and more interested in you.

So much of what we call communication is self-focused. The emphasis is on the "I." We com–mun–**I**–cate. But emphasizing the "I" destroys the correct pronunciation. If I want to speak correctly, I must remember that the emphasis belongs on "U."

Now that you have completed the first four days of week 1, can you identify four ways in which the process of managing your speech can be compared to navigating a ship? (Hint: the four daily lesson titles should help you remember). Review them on page 6.

Memorize at least the first sentence of your Breath Freshener (p. 6). Use the review card on page 147. Carry it with you as you go about your daily tasks or post it in a place you will see often.

Prepare your spirit for day 5, when you will be asked to evaluate your speech. Ask God to give you openness to seeing your speech from His vantage point.

Today's Tongue Tonic deals with accepting responsibility. Just as a ship's captain is responsible for the way he maneuvers his vessel, so you are responsible for the words that come out of your mouth. Demonstrate that you accept responsibility by using "I" statements when you speak.

Accept Responsibility

An important step to becoming an effective communicator is accepting responsibility for the part of the communication loop that belongs to you. Do not attempt to control the part that does not belong to you. When you expect and demand that the other person think or behave the way you want her to, you claim ownership for a part of the loop that is not yours and enter into a power struggle with her. The net result is conflict and miscommunication.

Healthy communication can only take place when each person accepts responsibility for his or her own part of the loop (see Matt. 12:36-37 on p. 20). Taking responsibility for your part of the loop means becoming aware of how your personality, feelings, attitudes, assumptions, habits, past experiences, and current environment affect the way you encode and decode messages (see page 15). It means carefully observing all the parts of the other person's message–verbal, vocal, and visual–and observing your own behavior to seek to be clear and consistent in the messages you send. Being responsible for your part of the loop means that you bear sole responsibility for what you think and say. No matter what the other person says or does, remind yourself, "I choose how I respond. I am responsible for me."

"I" Statements Own It

The best way to indicate that you take responsibility for your part of the loop and not for the other person's is to use "I" rather than "you" statements. When you start your thought with "I"–"I think … I feel … I see … I notice … I assume… I interpret …"–you demonstrate ownership of your thoughts, feelings, behavior, and interpretations. This decreases the chance that you will come across as judgmental or combative in your speech and increases the other person's receptiveness to your message.

Day Five

Taking Our Bearings
Tools help determine our position.

"We all stumble in many ways. If anyone is never at fault in what he says, he is a perfect man, able to keep his whole body in check."
James 3:2

Recently, the captain of a Greek ferry put his instruments on autopilot as his ship sailed toward the Aegean island of Paros. Captains are required to man the bridge for the last 11 kilometers approaching port, but he had sailed this route 6 to 8 times a week without incident. Confident of the autopilot settings, the captain took a nap while the first officer and crew left the bridge to watch a soccer match on television.

Three kilometers from Paros, the ship crashed into a rocky islet and sank. The islet was clearly marked with a light beacon; no attentive seaman would have missed it. But the captain was sleeping and unaware that his autopilot was steering the ship toward disaster. Sixty-six lives were lost. The captain and crew were charged with murder, neglect of duty, and violation of maritime procedures.

How foolish of that captain to depend on an autopilot setting without periodically checking to ensure that his vessel was staying on course. Yet how often do we do the same thing? We rely on our tongue's autopilot setting and fail to check whether we are headed in the right direction. To avoid disaster, we need to periodically take our bearings.

As we saw in the video, tools for checking our bearings include our conscience, feedback from others, and the conviction of the Holy Spirit. In today's lesson, you will be answering the Twenty Questions to check whether you are on course with God's plan for your speech. You can use the tools to help you answer the questions. Listen to your conscience. Consider the feedback that you have received from others. You may even want to ask your spouse or a good friend to go through the questions with you. Above all, pray and ask God to show you any areas in which you need to make adjustments.

When you can't change the direction of the wind, adjust your sails.
—Max DePree[3]

Twenty Questions

1. Do you gossip? Do you enjoy repeating the latest news or rumor you heard about another person? (see Prov. 11:13; 20:19; 26:20).
   ❏ never ❏ seldom ❏ occasionally ❏ often ❏ habitually

2. Do you slander? Do you say things about others behind their backs that you would not say to their faces? Do your words cast others in a less than positive light? (see Ps. 50:20; 52:4; Prov. 11:9).
   ❏ never ❏ seldom ❏ occasionally ❏ often ❏ habitually

3. Do you nag? Do you repeat your desires and opinions to others until you get what you want? (see Prov. 21:19; 26:21).
❏ never ❏ seldom ❏ occasionally ❏ often ❏ habitually

4. Do you meddle? Do you make the interaction between other people your concern? Do you try to referee arguments or act as a go-between? (see Prov. 26:17).
❏ never ❏ seldom ❏ occasionally ❏ often ❏ habitually

5. Do you brag? Do you seek to present your skills, your experiences or your accomplishments as greater than they really are? (see Prov. 14:23; 25:27; 27:2)
❏ never ❏ seldom ❏ occasionally ❏ often ❏ habitually

6. Do you lie? Are you ever less than truthful? Are you less than totally honest? Do you misrepresent yourself, others, or events? (see Ps. 120:3; 34:13; Prov. 12:19,22; 26:18-19; Eph. 4:15,25).
❏ never ❏ seldom ❏ occasionally ❏ often ❏ habitually

7. Are you quarrelsome? Do you feel a need to be proved right or to have the last word? Do you argue? (see Prov. 17:14; 20:3; 26:21; 27:15; Phil. 2:14).
❏ never ❏ seldom ❏ occasionally ❏ often ❏ habitually

8. Do you respond in anger? Are you hot-tempered or defensive? Are you easily provoked? (see Prov. 15:1; 29:11,22; Eph. 4:26-27).
❏ never ❏ seldom ❏ occasionally ❏ often ❏ habitually

9. Do you talk too much? Do you babble? Do you spend a lot of time on the phone or in chat rooms? Do you monopolize conversations with your opinions? Do you interrupt? (see Eccl. 10:11; Prov. 15:28; 29:20; Jas. 1:19).
❏ never ❏ seldom ❏ occasionally ❏ often ❏ habitually

10. Are you reluctant to admit you are wrong? Do you fail to ask forgiveness? Do you refuse to admit your error when you feel the other person's error is greater? (see Prov. 29:23; Jas. 5:16).
❏ never ❏ seldom ❏ occasionally ❏ often ❏ habitually

11. Do you betray a confidence? Do you repeat matters that you should keep private? If someone has failed or injured you, do you feel compelled to tell someone else about it? (see Prov. 6:19; 17:19; 19:11; 25:9-10)
❏ never ❏ seldom ❏ occasionally ❏ often ❏ habitually

12. Do you criticize? Do you find fault? Do you focus on the bad instead of the good? Do you see people's shortcomings more

than their strengths? (see Ps. 41:5; Rom. 1:30).
❑ never ❑ seldom ❑ occasionally ❑ often ❑ habitually

13. Do you complain? Do you bewail the circumstances you find yourself in? Do you let others know that you resent being inconvenienced? (see Phil. 2:14).
❑ never ❑ seldom ❑ occasionally ❑ often ❑ habitually

14. Do you make assumptions and assume the worst about other people's motives and intentions? (see 1 Tim. 6:3-4; Prov. 29:20).
❑ never ❑ seldom ❑ occasionally ❑ often ❑ habitually

15. Do you hold grudges? Do you bring up or focus on past wrongs? Do you accuse others? (see Prov. 11:12).
❑ never ❑ seldom ❑ occasionally ❑ often ❑ habitually

16. Are you sarcastic? Do you mock others? Do you use negative humor to put others down? (see Prov. 21:24; 9:7; 26:18-19).
❑ never ❑ seldom ❑ occasionally ❑ often ❑ habitually

17. Are you malicious? Are your words intended to cut and wound? Are your words harsh? (see Prov. 11:12; 17:4; 15:1; 16:27).
❑ never ❑ seldom ❑ occasionally ❑ often ❑ habitually

18. Are you insincere in your compliments? Do you flatter others for your own advantage? (see Prov. 26:28; 29:5).
❑ never ❑ seldom ❑ occasionally ❑ often ❑ habitually

19. Is your speech filthy? Do you swear or use foul language? Do you use the latest slang or crass expressions? (see Prov. 4:24; 10:31-32; Col. 3:8).
❑ never ❑ seldom ❑ occasionally ❑ often ❑ habitually

20. Do you fail to listen? Do you jump to conclusions before you are sure that you have heard and understood? (see Prov. 18:13; 19:20; Jas. 1:19).
❑ never ❑ seldom ❑ occasionally ❑ often ❑ habitually

Look back over your answers. Circle the numbers beside the three main areas in which your speech needs improvement.

James 3:2 says that when it comes to our speech "we all stumble in many ways." Nobody stays on course perfectly. But the mark of a good captain is his or her ability to identify when the vessel is off course and to make adjustments. In identifying the areas in which your speech needs improvement, you are taking the first step toward getting back on course.

If you look at a Canadian dime, you will find an image of Canada's most famous sailing vessel, the *Bluenose*. The *Bluenose* was constructed strongly to weather the rigorous challenges of North Atlantic fishing but was built also for speed. In 1921, she captured the International Fishermen's Trophy in a fierce competition between the best schooners in the world. She remained undefeated throughout her 18-year career.

The captain of the *Bluenose* faced the same challenges of every seaman: wind, waves, squalls, storms, sandbars, reefs, and treacherous rocky shorelines; but he knew how to harness the power of navigation to guide his ship to victory. If you follow God's plan for your speech, you, too, will weather the rigorous challenges of life's seas, harness the power of navigation, and cross the finish line in victory.

The 20 questions helped you take your bearings to identify where your speech needs adjustment. Read today's Tongue Tonic to see if your attitude toward communication also needs adjustment.

[1] Vine, W.E., *Vine's Expository Dictionary of Old and New Testament Words* (Grand Rapids, MI: Fleming H. Revell Co., 1981), 1078.
[2] Based on research by Dr. Albert Mehrabian, UCLA, as cited in Bert Decker, *The Art of Communicating* (Menlo Park, CA: Crisp Publications, Inc., 1996), 10-11.
[3] John Mason, *Don't Wait for Your Ship to Come In … Swim Out to Meet It!* (Tulsa, OK: Honor Books, 1994), 63.

Adjust Your Attitude

Humans are not mind readers, and we are not all-knowing. Adjusting our attitudes to be open to learn from others—even those with whom we disagree—is an important step towards effective communication.

An effective communicator is acutely aware of the complexity of the communication loop, her own limitations, and the potentials for miscommunication. She realizes that she is susceptible to misinterpreting the other person's behavior. She is open to the possibility that she might be wrong or that her behavior might be sending an inconsistent message, so she relies on feedback to confirm or correct the way she is decoding and encoding (see p. 15).

For example, Sally observes that Fred is speaking to her with a raised voice. Instead of assuming that he is angry, she checks out her decoding by asking: "I notice you are speaking with a raised voice. Are you feeling angry?"

"No," Fred responds in surprise, "My ears are plugged because I'm getting a cold—I didn't realize I was raising my voice. I'll speak more quietly." If Sally had not asked for Fred's feedback, she would have drawn the wrong conclusion. If Fred hadn't heard Sally's observation, he would have remained oblivious to how other people were interpreting his behavior. Sally changed her decoding, and Fred changed his encoding and behavior as a result of the exchange. They both learned (see Prov. 27:17).

The Power of Cause and Effect
Problems with the mouth originate in the heart.

Week Two

The Bible teaches that our words are connected to what is in our hearts. Reforming our words without reforming our hearts can't bring about lasting change. This week, harness the power of cause and effect to powerfully transform your speech from the ground of your heart up.

When we look at a plant, the stems and leaves we see above the surface are connected to the soil that lies beneath the surface. In this week's Talk Show you'll discover the cause and effect relationship between the soil of your heart and the fruit of your mouth.

Day 1: Growing from the Ground Up
   Words spring up from the ground of our hearts.
Day 2: Getting to the Root
   Healthy speech requires a healthy root.
Day 3: Digging Up Some Dirt
   The soil of deceit is a powerful contaminant.
Day 4: Analyzing the Soil
   Wise gardeners evaluate the quality of their soil.
Day 5: Turning Over the Sod
   The cleanup project begins with repentance.

This Week's Tongue Tonics:
   • Active Listening
   • Listening Barriers
   • Ineffective Listening Habits
   • Love to Listen
   • Layers of Meaning
   • Motivating Concerns

   • Unpack Your Presuppositions
   • Recognize Differences

"May the words of my mouth and the meditation of my heart be pleasing in your sight, O Lord, my Rock and my Redeemer" (Ps. 19:14).

Cut out the verse reminder on page 147. Post it or carry it with you.

The Power of Cause and Effect: It starts in the heart.

Matthew 12:33-35; 15:16-20

This Talk Show guide will help you follow the video for Session Two.

1. Look under the surface (see Matt. 15:18).

The words we speak are connected to what lies in our _____.

If the heart is bad, the words or actions are also bad, regardless of how they look to observers.

Words and behavior are connected to the attitudes and thoughts that are rooted in the deepest beliefs and values of our hearts.

2. Examine the quality of the soil (see Jer. 9:1-6; Isa. 5:20).

The soil is the _____ of everything we say and do.

Two types of soil:

• Soil of _____

• Soil of _____

Deceit is refusing to _____ God.

The quality of my speech will depend upon the type of _____ in which my words are anchored.

3. Initiate change from the bottom up (see Rom. 12:2).

Have you committed to a purification plan? ❑ Yes ❑ No

As the soil improves, good thoughts and attitudes will take root and sprout into healthy, beautiful, fruitful words. That's the power of cause and effect!

Day One

Growing from the Ground Up
Words spring from the ground of our hearts.

"Above all else, guard your heart, for it is the wellspring of life."
Proverbs 4:23

Last Valentine's Day I found a heart-shaped vase containing a fragrant, pink calla lily on the kitchen table. My husband had placed it there the night before. Later, I returned to my bedroom to discover a huge heart-shaped cookie on the pillow. Then I went to my office and saw a third surprise: a mysterious package with a cute heart-encircled teddy bear on the front. It contained a much-desired exercise outfit. (Just the thing I needed after eating that huge cookie!)

Heart-shaped objects symbolize love because we regard the heart as the center of our emotions. We are presented with the romantic notion that our emotions act independently from the rest of our being. According to this theory, we can mindlessly and blindly "fall in love." Our hearts can take us places our minds don't want to go.

This popular thought differs from the biblical imagery of the heart. In Hebrew and Greek, the term *heart* is used to describe "the center of things." When used of humans, it refers to the sum total of a person's physical, intellectual, and psychological attributes, and, more specifically, to the governing center of these attributes. According to the Bible, our heart is that part of us that makes us who we are. It is what directs all of our emotions as well as all of our thoughts, intents, and actions.

Our Words Spring from Our Hearts

"For out of the overflow of the heart the mouth speaks."
Matthew 12:34

When I look at a reflection of my face, I see the physical features that identify me: the shape of my nose, my eyebrows, the color of my eyes, the scar on my chin (from skydiving in my sleep from the top bunk onto the cement floor at a youth retreat). In the same way, when I look at my heart, I see all the spiritual features that identify who I am. My heart reflects my character, my thoughts, my desires, my emotions, my motivations, and the decisions I make.

In Proverbs 27:19, what two things function like a mirror?
❏ polished bronze
❏ still water
❏ the heart
❏ shined shoes

The Hebrew word for *reflect* means "to speak, answer, respond, testify." My face speaks of who I am physically just as my heart speaks of who I am spiritually. My words merely give an external voice to the internal speech of my heart.

In the box to the left, draw (or describe) the image that comes to mind when you think of the word *overflow*.

The image that comes to my mind is the water gurgling up from various underground mineral springs in the beautiful Canadian Rocky Mountains, our summer vacation spot. The water normally stays hidden underground, as part of the water table. But in certain areas it bubbles to the surface and overflows.

In each case, the overflow reveals what is hidden. The water comes up hot, cold, or stained depending on conditions below the surface. It's the same way with our words. Kind, pure words indicate a kind, pure heart. Words that are ugly point to ugliness within. Our hearts represent the ground from which our words spring (see Prov. 4:23).

"The words of a man's mouth are deep waters, but the fountain of wisdom is a bubbling brook."
Proverbs 18:4

Good Hearts Produce Good Fruit

Read Matthew 12:33-35. Circle the picture that illustrates the analogy Jesus used in verse 33:

What is the first and most important criterion for harvesting good fruit from your mouth?

"Make a tree good and its fruit will be good, or make a tree bad and its fruit will be bad, for a tree is recognized by its fruit."
Matthew 12:33

In order to harvest good fruit from your mouth, you must "make" the tree of your heart "good." The Greek verb for *make* means "to form, produce, bring about." The particular tense of this verb refers to a completed action. Read today's Word from the Word (on the next page) to discover what it means to make your heart's tree good.

[good] MAKING YOUR TREE "GOOD"

The biblical meaning of the term *good* is "acceptable, beautiful, pleasing; morally excellent–a perfect inward nature that manifests and demonstrates itself outwardly." Making the tree of our lives good means bringing it in line with God's standard–having our hearts made beautiful, acceptable, perfect, and morally excellent.

How does this transformation take place? If you are not sure, turn to page 48 and read "Beginning a Relationship with Jesus." If you pray the prayer to enter into a relationship with Jesus as Savior and Lord, or if you are unsure of your relationship with Jesus, call your pastor, group leader, or another Christian friend today. He or she will be glad to suggest some next steps.

Trees take time to grow and mature. I have an apple tree in my backyard that struggled for three years before it produced even one apple. The next summer, it produced five or six, and the next year, a few more. Even though it will occasionally produce a deformed or underdeveloped apple, the tendency to bear good fruit is there and increasing yearly. As a result, I consider it to be a good tree.

When you enter into a relationship with Jesus, the tree of your heart is made good. That means that the inclination of your heart has changed toward producing good fruit. In spite of this, you may still struggle with bad speech and bad behavior. You may feel frustrated because you don't see the harvest coming quickly enough. Remember, just like my apple tree, it may take some time for you to mature. But it is the *tendency toward productive growth* that indicates that your heart has changed and you are on the right track.

> He hath a heart as sound as a bell, and his tongue is the clapper; for what his heart thinks his tongue speaks.
> —Shakespeare, Much Ado about Nothing

If the tree of your heart has been made good but you are struggling with bad speech, what might be the problem? (See Matt. 12:35.)

❏ I am surrounded by irritating people who make me angry.
❏ My circumstances are unbearable.
❏ My parents were poor role models.
❏ I am tired and overly sensitive.
❏ I have not "stored up" enough good in my heart.

To *store up* means "to collect, accumulate or stock something as a reserve for future use; to lay up or put away." A couple of years ago, I set up a pantry downstairs in our storage room. Every time I went shopping for groceries, I bought a few extra supplies. Over time, the pantry became very well stocked.

Now I am confident that I have the necessary reserves to manage the hearty appetites of my teenage boys. No more rushing to the corner grocery store in a panic because I have run out of something.

When we speak, particularly in unplanned situations of being irritated, tired, sensitive, or stressed, we reach down into the pantry of our hearts and bring out what has been stored up over time. Words spring from the ground of our hearts. If we have stored up good in our hearts, our words will be good. If we haven't, or if our stores are meager, we may not have the resources available.

Even the most well-stocked pantry will run out of supplies if it is not regularly re-stocked. Do you need to work on improving your "storage" habits? What can you do this week to "store up" more goodness in your heart? One way is to keep the weekly Breath Freshener on the tip of your tongue. Begin memorizing that verse found on page 28 today.

This week's Tongue Tonics will teach you to listen, observe, and look under the surface of words to hear the message of the heart.

Active Listening

Listening is an active process involving more than just the ears. The Chinese character for the verb *to listen* contains the symbols for ears, eyes, heart, and undivided attention. Active listening means giving our undivided attention–hearing with our ears, observing carefully with our eyes, and understanding with our hearts.

Listening Barriers

The average person speaks between 100 and 150 words per minute but thinks up to 600 words per minute. As a result, our minds have a lot of spare time to use while others are talking. Use this time to focus on understanding the speaker's ideas. Otherwise, you will create listening barriers such as:

Running Ahead—thinking about what you are going to say next; planning a rebuttal.
Wandering Off—being pre-occupied, thinking about personal interests, or daydreaming.
Jumping In—interrupting the other person's thoughts to interject your own.
Brushing Away—mentally categorizing the speaker's thoughts as unimportant or insignificant without duly considering them or assuming you already understand his or her perspective.
Blocking Out—refusing to acknowledge the topic the other person is addressing, selectively filtering the message to block out portions.

Getting to the Root
Healthy speech requires a healthy root.

"I will sprinkle clean water on you, and you will be clean; I will cleanse you from all your impurities and from all your idols. I will give you a new heart and put a new spirit in you; I will remove from you your heart of stone and give you a heart of flesh. And I will put my Spirit in you and move you to follow my decrees and be careful to keep my laws."
Ezekiel 36:25-27

My African violet looked sick. Many leaves had curled and darkened; a few appeared translucent and jelly-like. The flowers, which had once bloomed vibrant purple, had all but died. Not having inherited my mother's green thumb, I assumed that tiny insects were to blame. I generously sprayed the leaves with a can of bug killer.

A few days later, the violet looked worse than ever. It was time to call in the expert. Hearing the symptoms, my mom quickly diagnosed the ailment: Root Rot. *Root Rot?* Not bugs?

Root Rot is caused by a variety of fungi that infest the soil and attack the roots of plants and trees. As the disease progresses, black and brown lesions develop on the crown of the plant and the leaves begin to rot. Treating the disease in potted houseplants holds some hope, but in nature a cure is difficult. Root Rot is normally fatal.

The Connection Between the Mouth and Heart

I had an inverted perspective on what was causing the problem for my violet. I thought the problem originated in the leaves. In today's lesson, we will be reading about some people who had an inverted perspective on the connection between the mouth and the heart. They believed that the mouth could contaminate the heart. Jesus showed that their approach was faulty. He taught that the heart contained the root of contamination. The heart and the mouth are indeed connected, but the flow of contamination goes from the heart to the mouth and not the other way around.

Read Mark 7:1-23. The Pharisees were a Jewish sect noted for their strict interpretation and observance of religious law and for their pretensions of superior sanctity. In verse 2, what were the Pharisees concerned about?

_____

Did Jesus share their opinion? ❑ Yes ❑ No
According to Jesus, how do people become unclean?
❑ failing to wash their hands
❑ petting the dog
❑ allowing evil to take root in their hearts
❑ wearing yesterday's clothes

Why the big argument about cleanliness? Didn't Jesus think it was important to wash His hands before eating? Didn't He know that germs on the hands could be ingested and cause severe illness? In Jesus' mind, and in the mind of the Pharisees, the issue at stake was much larger than bacteria. To understand what it was, we need to understand the biblical significance of *clean* and *unclean.*

The Greek word for *unclean* comes from the word *common,* meaning "that which is unhindered in contact and exposure." Clean, on the other hand, refers to "that which has been purified, set apart and devoted to God." To the Jews, "clean" meant holy. The unclean was common, whereas the clean was special; like the difference between the bowls you put on the table every day and your antique bone china. The fine china is reserved—set apart. It is not for daily use.

Jews in an unclean condition were disqualified from taking part in worship. They became ceremonially unclean through contact with mildew, infection, disease, death, blood, or bodily discharge. An individual who had become defiled in this manner could be restored to a clean condition through the specified washing and the offering of sacrifices. Certain foods were also considered unclean and thus prohibited—pork, for example. For Jews, adhering to cleanliness rules was an expression of devotion to God (see Lev. 10:10-11). By symbolically making themselves holy, the Israelites were allowed to approach and enjoy a relationship with a holy God (see Lev. 11:44).

A cup brimful of sweet water cannot spill even one drop of bitter water however suddenly jolted.
—Amy Carmichael

If cleanliness symbolized holiness, why wasn't Jesus pleased with the Pharisee's standards? (see Mark 7:13).

According to Old Testament law, the priests were required to wash their hands and feet prior to entering the Tabernacle (see Ex. 30:19; 40:13) and wash their hands before eating sacrificial food (see Num. 18:8-13). Over time, however, the religious leaders had extended this rite to include all of the people of Israel and had so precisely defined the process of hand washing that the amount of water, the posture of the hands, and even the direction of the flowing water were strictly regulated. One's complete cleansing and consequent spirituality depended upon perfect attention to details.

The importance the religious leaders placed on such ceremonial washings is reflected in the fact that a major section of the Jewish *Mishna, Tohoroth,* which means "cleanness," is dedicated to this subject. The instructions were meant to protect God's Word, but had grown so complex that they concealed the intent of the original directives. The tradition thus nullified the Word of God.

External Cleanness vs. Internal Purity

In being obsessed with external washing, the religious leaders had totally twisted the intent of the practice. They had confused external cleanness of the hands and mouth with internal purity of heart. Jesus taught that we are not defiled by what we eat, even when our hands are not properly washed. The capacity for fellowship with God is not destroyed by uncleanness of food or hands–it is destroyed by sin.

When Jesus died to pay the penalty for our sins, the need for these external symbols of holiness–ceremonial purification and abstaining from unclean foods–changed (see Heb. 9:13-14). In overturning them, Jesus did not negate the demand for purity. Rather, He sharpened it. His standards went way beyond the standards of the Pharisees. The Pharisees merely demanded that things were done right on the outside. Jesus, however, taught that things must first be right on the inside. According to Jesus, external symbols of holiness–doing the right things and saying the right words–are of no worth if the thoughts and attitudes of our hearts are not right.

> *"Woe to you, teachers of the law and Pharisees, you hypocrites! You clean the outside of the cup and dish, but inside they are full of greed and self-indulgence. Blind Pharisee! First clean the inside of the cup and dish, and then the outside also will be clean."*
> Matthew 23:25-26

Read Matthew 23:25-26. The outside of the Pharisee's cup and dish were clean. On the diagram, record what was on the inside:

In verse 26, what did Jesus say the Pharisees needed to do?
❑ Get a new set of dishes.
❑ Change their brand of detergent.
❑ Clean the inside first.
❑ Buy a dishwasher.

How does Jesus' advice in verse 26, "First clean the inside of the cup and dish, and then the outside also will be clean" relate to our speech? When the thoughts and attitudes of our hearts are clean and pure, our words will also be clean and pure. Jesus wants to clean us up on the inside so that what is on the outside will also sparkle.

As the thoughts and attitudes rooted in your heart become clean and more pleasing, your words will also increase in beauty. That's His promise. And that's the power of cause and effect!

Ineffective Listening Habits

Do you recognize the following types of listening patterns?

Assuming Alice assumes that she knows what you think and feel. Alice could finish all your sentences. She does not hear when you offer new or different information.

Defensive Dana is distrustful and touchy. She sees your remarks as personal attacks. Dana perceives that you are out to get her, so she's closed to hearing anything you have to say about her behavior.

Ambushing Amanda appears to listen carefully, but only because she is collecting information with which to attack you. She hears your words, but her goal is to use them later as ammunition.

Self-centered Samantha manages to turn any conversation into an opportunity to showcase her own accomplishments and perspectives. All that matters to Sam is that you know what she thinks.

Solution Sally knows how to fix everything. Before she has even heard you out, she knows what you ought to do.

Denying Darla denies the significance of situations and your right to your feelings. "You shouldn't feel that way" and "Don't make such a big deal out of it" are her mottos.

Love to Listen

Effective communicators working at LISTEN-ing skills:

Limit Your Lip: By talking less you give the other person the opportunity to express his or her thoughts. A philosopher once said, "We have been given two ears and but a single mouth, in order that we may hear more and talk less."

Identify Key Issues: Effective listeners use their "spare thinking time" to extract the main thought from the speaker's words and behavior. They ask themselves questions such as: "How does he feel?" "What does this mean to her?"

Silence Distractions: Listening distractions can be external—ringing cell phones and doorbells, radio, TV, or other conversations—or internal—preoccupation with other thoughts, fatigue, and/or stress. Effective listeners do everything possible to silence the internal and external distractions that can hinder their ability to listen.

Table Conclusions: Most of us are guilty of making snap judgments. This temptation is the greatest when the speaker's ideas differ from our own. Instead of exchanging ideas, conversations turn into verbal combat with "opponents" trying to conquer and claim victory for their point of view. Effective listeners table their conclusions until they understand the speaker's point of view.

Echo and Inquire: Effective listeners check to make sure they are decoding the speaker's thoughts and feelings accurately by reflecting their understanding back to the speaker for verification (echo), and by asking questions (inquire). They do not conclude that they understand until the speaker clarifies and verifies the listener's decoding.

Negate Defensiveness: The listener's goal in this step is to understand the speaker's perspective—what the speaker thinks and feels and why he or she feels that way. The goal is not to defend, give a rebuttal, or counterattack. Effective listeners receive messages nondefensively.

Digging Up Some Dirt

The soil of deceit is a powerful contaminant.

"I will build them up and not tear them down; I will plant them and not uproot them. I will give them a heart to know me, that I am the Lord. They will be my people, and I will be their God, for they will return to me with all their heart."
Jeremiah 24:6-7

Root Rot infects plants through a fungus that thrives under soggy soil conditions. The fungus reproduces and forms spores in the soil. Even if the soil dries out, dormant spores are easily reactivated by moisture. Curing a plant of Root Rot therefore requires more than just treating the leaves, stems, and roots. It requires that the soil be removed and replaced. You can't really beat the disease without changing the soil in which the plant is grounded.

It's the same way with us. We can try to change our negative words and behavior—or even try to uproot wrong attitudes and thoughts—but we can't really beat the disease until we change the false beliefs and values deep in the ground of our hearts.

In this week's Talk Show, we talked about how our words can be compared to a plant. See if you can fill in the blanks of the diagram. If not, read the paragraph below.

leaves/fruit = _____

root = _____

soil = _____

Beliefs and Values

Our words and behavior are like the leaves of a plant. They are above the surface and can be observed. Our attitudes and thoughts are hidden like the root of a plant. Some roots of bad speech are envy, pride, malice, arrogance, bitterness, and lack of self-control. Just as in the case of my African violet, a third factor affects the plant. It is the most important factor: the soil. The soil represents our deepest beliefs and values.

Soil conditions determine what kind of plants will grow and whether or not those plants will be healthy. The soil creates an environment in the heart in which either goodness or evil will flourish. The soil is the foundation—the ground motivator—of everything we say and do. In the Talk Show, we learned that two types of soil can exist in the human heart: the pure soil of truth and the contaminated soil of deceit. Let's find out more about these two soil conditions.

Read the following verses and match each reference to the thought it presents:

Psalm 50:19-20   "The heart is deceitful above all things."
Isaiah 5:18   Those who don't listen to the Lord are deceitful.
Isaiah 30:9   Sin is drawn along by "cords of deceit."
Jeremiah 17:9   Deceit harnesses and directs the tongue.

According to Jeremiah 17:9, deceit is the predominant condition of the human heart|, but what is deceit? The dictionary defines *deceit* as "the concealment or perversion of truth for the purpose of misleading." The Bible gives other information about the nature of deceit.

Read Jeremiah 9:1-6. According to verses 3 and 6, what is the essence of deceit?

_____

The Bible explains that the essence of deceit is failing to acknowledge God. Deceit occurs whenever God's truth is concealed, perverted, or denied. A deceitful heart fails to acknowledge God. It does not believe God's words, value God's ways, think God's thoughts, or adopt the same attitude as God's heart. Our hearts are deceived whenever we are out of line with God.

The Bible has a lot to say about our mouths, our lips, our tongues, for our speech betrays us. What is down in the well will come up in the bucket.[1]—Vance Havner

Faulty Speech = Faulty Beliefs

The Bible clearly indicates that the soil of deceit is responsible for the evil that shows up in our words. Deceit allows evil in all its various forms—such as envy, pride, malice, and bitterness—to take root in our hearts and sprout out into what we say. In the following verses, circle the words and phrases that indicate how deceit affects the tongue.

"Your tongue plots destruction; it is like a sharpened razor, you who practice deceit. You love evil rather than good, falsehood rather than speaking the truth. You love every harmful word, O you deceitful tongue!" (Ps. 52:2-4)

"Their throats are open graves; their tongues practice deceit. The poison of vipers in on their lips. Their mouths are full of cursing and bitterness. Their feet are swift to shed blood; ruin and misery mark their ways, and the way of peace they do not know." (Rom. 3:13-17)

Let's look at a practical example. We'll evaluate the speech problem, identify the root attitude, and see if we can identify the false belief from which it sprang.

"You are so stupid!" Sally screamed, after Fred had forgotten that it was his turn to pick the kids up from school. "You never get anything right! I wish I had never married such a blundering, inconsiderate, stupid fool!"

speech	criticism, mocking, exaggeration, put-downs
root attitudes	impatience, anger, bitterness
false beliefs	I know his motives.**Truth:** Only God can see the heart (see 1 Chron. 28:9) I am better than he. **Truth:** All have sinned, me included (see Rom. 3:23). I have the right to judge him. **Truth:** God alone is judge (see Rom. 14:10). I have the right to be resentful. **Truth:** God says forgive (see Matt. 18:21-22).

Can you come up with your own example? Choose a recent situation in which you or someone else spoke substandard words. Describe the situation:

_____

_____

Now evaluate it in the blank chart below.

speech	. . . .
root attitudes	. . . .
false beliefs	

Can you see how faulty speech is connected to faulty beliefs? Over the next few weeks, as you notice faulty words or behavior in your life, ask God to help you dig down to unearth the tainted soil beneath. All of us have deceit in our hearts. But, thankfully, God has promised to purify our heart's soil (see Heb. 10:16-18). Close today's lesson by thanking God for His commitment to help us purify the soil of our hearts. Write your prayer in the margin.

Today's Tongue Tonic helps us understand the layers of meaning and motivating concerns that are attached to interpersonal messages.

Layers of Meaning

Person-to-person messages normally contain two layers of meaning. **Manifest meaning** consists of the visible part (verbal, vocal, visual) of the message. Manifest meaning is linked to the specific interaction at hand. **Implicit meaning** is not readily apparent. It is implied. It consists of the person's view of the overall situation, the pattern of interacting that has been established, and the broader relationship between the speaker and listener.

For example, a woman may tell her boyfriend, "You're late!" The manifest meaning is that he arrived 45 minutes after she expected him. Implicitly, she might be angry that he disappointed her again, or worried that something had happened to him, or wondering why he hadn't called, or maybe even triumphant that he was late and she wasn't. Messages contain manifest and implicit meaning. To interpret the message correctly, the receiver must always seek to understand both of these layers.

Motivating Concerns

Four common concerns motivate the way people behave.
Control–sitting in the driver's rather than the passenger's seat. People want to feel safe, have their physical needs met, and make their own decisions. People with excessive needs for control try to control others instead of accepting that ultimately, individuals can only control their own actions and reactions.
Connection–the desire to feel loved, wanted, approved of, and accepted. Individuals desire to connect with others and feel included as part of a group.
Competence–feeling capable, and wanting others to recognize their gifts and abilities.
Contribution–having meaning and significance in their lives.

A helpful tool in communicating is identifying which concern primarily motivates you and which motivates the other person. For example, I may refuse a friend's lunch invitation because I do not feel I have the time that day (control). Her motivating concern may be quality time spent together (connection). I may need to assure her that I value her friendship and would enjoy meeting at another time.

Day Four

Analyzing the Soil
Wise gardeners evaluate the quality of their soil.

"Still other seed fell on good soil. It came up, grew and produced a crop, multiplying thirty, sixty, or even a hundred times."
Mark 4:8

Summers in western Canada are short. The snow doesn't usually melt until mid-April. By May, the trees and grass begin to blush green, slowly awakening from their winter sleep. As soon as the ground has dried, Brent sends the boys out to rake all the snow, mold, rotting leaves, and dead blades of grass from our lawn. He then applies fertilizer to the lawn to stimulate its growth.

All our neighbors do the same thing, but the lawn of one neighbor always greens the fastest. Not only does it turn green first, but also it turns a darker, lusher green than all the other lawns on the block—staying that way through the entire summer. Other lawns become blotchy or uneven, but this neighbor's lawn remains golf-green perfect in texture and color.

His secret? Soil testing. All the other neighbors buy standard nitrogen-based fertilizer to feed the grass. But this neighbor tests the soil to evaluate its composition. Based on his evaluation, he buys the appropriate nutrients to feed the soil. He understands that nutrient stresses and imbalances in the soil reduce plant vigor and increase a lawn's susceptibility to damage from drought, disease, insects, and other conditions. In testing the soil, he can determine the proper nutrient program for maximum turf building. His attention to soil quality means that he has a more luxurious lawn, more brilliant flowers, and denser foliage than anyone else in the neighborhood.

The Heart's Soil

Jesus was concerned about the quality of soil in a person's heart. He understood that the condition of the heart's soil is ultimately responsible for the condition of the plants that grow there.

Read the parable of the soils in Luke 8:4-15. Draw a line to connect the type of soil with its plant condition.

Hard Soil   Plant is healthy and bears fruit.

Rocky Soil   Plant is choked and does not mature.

Thorny Soil   No plant grows. Seeds are trampled or eaten by birds.

Good Soil   Plant withers in the heat.

Label each statement with the appropriate soil condition: hard, rocky, thorny, or good.

_____ 1. They are distracted by worries, riches and pleasures.

_____ 2. When things get difficult, they fall away.

_____ 3. They reject the message of the Bible.

_____ 4. They produce good fruit in their lives.

In the parable of the soils, the seed represents the Word of God. Another name for the *Word of God* is the "word of truth" (Eph. 1:13). God sows seeds of truth in the soil of our hearts. Whether or not that truth takes root and grows into healthy plants depends on the condition of our hearts' soil.

Estimate the percentage of your heart that falls into each soil category (total should equal 100 percent).

_____ % hard   _____ % rocky

_____ % thorny   _____ % good

There are a few reasons why I don't manage my lawn as well as my neighbor does. First, I feel I have too many other more important things to do. I don't want to change my priorities for the sake of greener grass. Second, I am content to match the standard of those around me. Many of our other neighbors |settle for "adequate" lawn care. Compared to the norm, I think my lawn looks pretty good. Finally, I am not willing to pay the price to have the soil tested and to purchase and apply the correct nutrients. It costs too much to follow the program year after year.

I think my reasons for failing to work at improving the condition of my lawn's soil are valid. Unfortunately, I often use the same reasons to justify settling for an adequate but not excellent condition for the soil of my heart: I am distracted by other priorities. Compared to everyone else, I think my heart looks pretty good, and I am unwilling to pay the price.

Yet when I compare the consequences of having a less-than-excellent lawn to the consequences of having a less-than-excellent heart, I see that these reasons aren't valid at all. Improving the condition of my heart ought to be my highest priority–regardless of what others do and regardless of the cost. I long for a 100 percent commitment to hearing, accepting, retaining, and applying God's truth.

"This is what the Lord says … 'Break up your unplowed ground and do not sow among thorns.'"
Jeremiah 4:3

Read Psalm 51:6. What does God want us to cultivate in the deepest part of our hearts?

_____

In Luke 8:12, Jesus identifies the Devil as the one who seeks to take away the word of truth from people's hearts. Read today's Word from the Word to find out more about this deceiving accuser.

[de.vil] THE DECEIVING ACCUSER

The word *devil* is derived from the Greek word *diabolos*, which is the root for the word *diabolic*. A *diabolos* is one who makes malicious false statements; a false accuser; a slanderer. In the Bible, the word is used 34 times as a title for Satan, the author of evil and enemy of God.

The Devil constantly makes malicious false statements about God, the ways of God, the Bible, and people. He slanders, accuses, perverts, and twists the truth. His primary goal is to deceive or entice people to believe falsehood and to reject the truth of God (see 2 Thess. 2:9-12; Rev. 20:7-8).

The Devil is the father of deception. There is no truth in him (see John 8:44). It was through deception that he enticed Eve to sin (see Gen. 3:13; 2 Cor. 11:3). He is "an enemy of everything that is right! ... full of all kinds of deceit and trickery ... perverting the right ways of the Lord" (Acts 13:10).

In contrast, all of God's "words are true" (Ps. 119:160). Christ claimed to be "the Truth" (John 14:6). He "committed no sin, and no deceit was found in his mouth" (1 Pet. 2:22).

Truth is characteristic of Christ. Deceit is characteristic of Satan. When we speak, we follow the example of one or the other.

Test the Heart's Soil

In order for the words of our mouths to be good, the soil of our heart must be good. It must be filled with the truth of God and emptied of false (deceitful) beliefs, values, attitudes, and thoughts. As we learned in yesterday's lesson, deceit is a condition of the heart that occurs whenever God's truth is concealed, perverted, or denied. Today we learned that this happens when we are distracted by life's worries, by the pursuit of riches, possessions, and pleasures. It can also happen when difficult circumstances overwhelm us or when we neglect or reject God's instructions.

The Old Testament records how the people of the nation of Israel struggled with maintaining a quality heart condition. The prophet Hosea challenged them to manage the ground of their hearts correctly so that they could harvest a bountiful, healthful crop.

Read Hosea 10:12-13. On the chart below contrast what the people of Israel should have been sowing with what they had been sowing in the garden of their hearts.

What Should Have Been Done (v. 12)	What Had Been Done (v. 13)
_____	_____
_____	_____
_____	_____

The Israelites made the mistake of relying on their own strength and resources to manage their ground. Hosea encouraged them to break up the hard ground and to seek the Lord, sowing His seed of truth in their hearts. Are you willing to do what the people of Israel failed to do? If so, ask God to test the soil of your heart and show you areas where it needs improvement.

Today's Tongue Tonic deals with unpacking our presuppositions which are ways our hearts can be deceived.

Unpack Your Presuppositions

Presuppositions affect the way you encode and decode messages (see p. 15). Presuppositions frame, box, and bias:

Frame: A frame defines the shape and boundary for everything it contains. We mentally frame people according to their physical characteristics, roles, personality, memberships, skills, and occupations. The frame affects our interpretation of his or her behavior. For instance, we may regard silence from someone we have framed as "shy" as a sign of insecurity, while the same behavior from someone we have framed as "outgoing" might be viewed as a sign of unfriendliness.

Box: A box defines our expectations of how an individual will think, act, or respond. For example: "He always gets angry." "She will never agree to it." Whenever we expect and anticipate certain behavior from others, we "box" them.

Bias: A negative bias attributes a negative behavior to a character flaw, while a positive bias attributes that same behavior to circumstance. For example, if James raises his voice, I believe he is an impatient person. But if Jack raises his voice, I believe he has been under a lot of pressure.

The frames, boxes, and biases we mentally assign to others can blind us to interpreting them correctly. We must be open to the possibility we have incorrectly categorized them or that they have changed. To gain true understanding, we must be willing to unpack and challenge our presuppositions.

Day Five

Turning Over the Sod
The cleanup project begins with repentance.

"Search me, O God, and know my heart; test me and know my anxious thoughts. See if there is any offensive way in me, and lead me in the way everlasting."
Psalm 139:23-24

It looked like any other recreational area. On any given day, dozens of adults and children played on the tennis courts, baseball field, and playground. Nestled in the midst of a growing suburban community, this three-acre park was a place of fun and laughter. But all was not well at Pepe Field. Under the surface, hazardous wastes were emitting toxic gases. The recreational area was situated on top of an old industrial site that for over 30 years had been used as a landfill for wastes from the manufacture of cleaning products.

As time passed, recreational users and residents began to complain about the odor of hydrogen sulfide in the park, so the town of Boonton, New Jersey, set up equipment to pump away and treat the leaching groundwater. The foul odor was reduced. For more than a decade, residents continued to use the park, but masking the smell didn't address the underlying problem. Unbeknown to park users, the hazardous wastes were emitting increasingly toxic gases. When the Environmental Protection Agency conducted soil tests in 1982, the site was closed to the public.

An Ineffective Disguise

The tranquility of the park had been deceptive. It had disguised the hazardous condition of the soil underneath. In the same way, a person's mouth can disguise what is in his or her heart.

Read Psalm 55:20-21. In the box on the left, draw what David's companion's speech looked like on the outside. In the box on the right, draw what was hidden in his heart.

The quality of our words is determined by what lies beneath. The Bible teaches that our words are judged according to the root and soil that anchors them. Even if the words look good, the root and soil can be contaminated. People who have pleasant-sounding words can have as much or even more of a speech problem than people whose words betray the evil in their hearts.

The Bible says words can cover a bad heart with a shiny, thin coating of veneer. Our lips conceal hatred (see Prov. 10:18), malice (Prov. 26:23-26), greed, self-indulgence, hypocrisy and all kinds of wickedness (see Matt. 23:25-28). Just like Pepe Field, what is underneath the surface eventually will come up—in one way or another.

"Like a coating of glaze over earthenware are fervent lips with an evil heart."
Proverbs 26:23

What principle does Galatians 6:7-9 teach about what we put in the ground of our hearts? (Check one.)
❑ A penny saved is a penny earned.
❑ Cleanliness is next to godliness.
❑ Time heals all hurts.
❑ We reap what we sow.

God is not deceived. Nothing in all creation is hidden from His sight (see Heb. 4:13). The Bible tells us that "the Lord searches every heart and understands every motive behind the thoughts" (1 Chron. 28:9; see also Ps. 7:9). He hears every word, sees every thought, knows every attitude, and examines every belief. Our "guilt is not hidden from" Him (Ps. 69:5).

Read 1 John 1:8-10. If we claim we have no sin, who are we deceiving? Underline the statement.

If I make this claim, what does this indicate about me? (Check all that apply.)
❑ I am misled.   ❑ God's Word has no place in my life.
❑ The truth is not in me.   ❑ I believe God is a liar.

Did you check all the boxes? Psalm 36:1-2 says that one of the prime characteristics of a wicked person is that "in his own eyes he flatters himself too much to detect or hate his sin." Do you fail to detect or hate the sin in your life? Do you flatter yourself into believing that the condition of your heart is not too bad?

We tend to think our words and hearts are pretty good—especially when we compare ourselves to others. I know that in the past I have been proud of my ability to control my mouth. According to the Bible, my pride is an indication of the deceptiveness of my heart. Like the residents of Boonton, I ignore the foul odor in the air or try to minimize the smell and continue to play the game—unaware of the dangers of the hazardous waste percolating under the surface. If I stop and take a good look, I see that my heart is full of sin. I need help to clean it up.

"If we claim to be without sin, we deceive ourselves and the truth is not in us. If we confess our sins, he is faithful and just and will forgive us our sins and purify us from all unrighteousness. If we claim we have not sinned, we make him out to be a liar and his word has no place in our lives."
1 John 1:8-10

An Effective Solution

In 1980 Congress established a multibillion-dollar program called the Superfund to identify and clean up hazardous waste sites across the United States. Pepe Field was one of the first Superfund sites identified. The Superfund program removed the contaminated soil and the park was restored and reopened in November of 2000.

The town's effort to manage the site by treating the noxious odor had been inadequate. Our efforts to manage the sin in our hearts will be inadequate. We need to call on God, the One who has the expertise and resources to clean our hearts from the inside out. It is a lifelong process. Proverbs 28:13 says, "He who conceals his sins does not prosper, but whoever confesses and renounces them finds mercy."

Reread 1 John 1:8-10 on page 47, and circle the phrase that indicates what God will do when we confess our sins to Him.

Take some time right now to confess your sins. Identify impurities in your speech and behavior, in your thoughts and attitudes, and in your beliefs and values. If you need help identifying some, refer to pages 24-26 (week 1, day 5). Pray and ask God to forgive you. He has promised that He will. If you have not made a commitment to Jesus as your personal Lord and Savior, the place to begin is confessing your need of Him. Read below how to begin that relationship.

Beginning a Relationship with Jesus

The Bible tells us that we all fall short of the goodness of God (see Rom. 3:23). Even the good we are able to do is like filthy rags in comparison to Him (see Isa. 64:6). Because of His righteous nature, God has no choice but to condemn us for our failure to match His level of goodness (see Rom.6:23). We all deserve to be punished.

God's remedy for this impossible situation was to send His Son Jesus to be our substitute, bearing the penalty for evil in our stead (see Rom. 3:10). Jesus Christ's death on the cross was a gift of love from God the Father (see Rom. 5:8). Entering into a relationship with Jesus is the only way that our hearts can meet God's standard (see John 14:6; 2 Cor. 5:17). *Justification* means that by virtue of our acceptance of Christ's sacrifice, God the Father accepts and adopts us as His children.

When we commit to a relationship with Jesus as Savior and Lord, God sends His Spirit into our hearts to give us His new nature. As we cooperate with His Spirit, He transforms us from the inside out for the rest of our lives. *Sanctification* refers to the lifelong process of becoming more like Jesus—maturing and bearing good fruit.

Are you confident that you have entered into a relationship with Jesus? If you have not, or if you are unsure of your relationship with Jesus, why don't you call your small-group leader, a Christian friend, or your pastor? They would be happy to pray with you.

In Hosea 14, Hosea outlined the results of repentance: God will heal us and pour out His dew upon us so we will "blossom like a lily," send down strong roots like cedars (v. 5), and "flourish like the grain" (v. 7). What an amazing picture! Purifying the soil of our hearts produces a bountiful harvest of

Man is born with his back toward God. When he truly repents, he turns right around and faces God. Repentance is a change of mind. ... Repentance is the tear in the eye of faith.
—D.L. Moody

fruit from our lips. A beautiful heart produces beautiful words. That's the power of cause and effect!

Today's Tongue Tonic deals with recognizing people's unique life experiences which affect their messages and how they communicate.

[1]Dennis J. Hester, comp., *The Vance Havner Quote Book* (Grand Rapids, MI: Baker Book House, 1986), 220.

Recognize Differences

We are unique individuals with unique life experiences. To understand the deeper meaning of someone's message, keep in mind the dimensions that contribute to our differing perspectives.

Personalities create differences in how we interact. A sanguine person (optimistic) will evaluate a situation very differently than a melancholic (sad).

Backgrounds and cultures create differences in how we view individuality, family, authority, relationships, nonverbal cues, time, and countless other topics. For example, Western cultures, which have a strong individualistic orientation, value assertiveness; in Asian cultures, with their greater collective group orientation, assertiveness is more likely to be regarded as rude.

Socioeconomic factors also have a powerful impact on our attitudes and behavior. The prosperity or poverty we may have experienced influences our expectations and ambitions.

Faith is a source of profound difference in people's most basic values, assumptions, and attitudes.

History and age also affect how we perceive relationships and interpersonal behavior. Someone who grew up during the depression could have a very different perspective on finances than someone who grew up during the baby boomer years.

Gender is an important consideration. Overall, men are more concerned with communicating information and facts, while women tend to communicate feelings.

Recognizing differences helps us interpret the meaning of someone's message or send a message they will understand. In most cases, it is not appropriate to battle over whose perspective is the right one. More often than not, the perspectives are merely different–not right and wrong. Finally, recognizing differences helps us to see how valuable others are and how much we need their input. In God's plan, our diversity contributes to commitment and unity.

The Power of Exchange

Fruitful speech requires exchanging bad habits for good.

This week, harness the power of exchange to sow seeds of good thoughts that will grow and fill the garden of your heart with beauty.

Mom's advice—"If you can't say anything good, don't say anything at all"—may keep us from sinning from our mouths, but it doesn't fill the void in our hearts. In this week's Talk Show, find out how King David learned to fill the empty space in his heart with goodness.

Day 1: Seeds of Truth
  Sow truth instead of falsehood.
Day 2: Seeds of Abundance
  Focus on what is received instead of what is owed.
Day 3: Seeds of Grace
  Be a grace-giver instead of a debt-counter.
Day 4: Seeds of Gratitude
  Be thankful instead of unthankful.
Day 5: Seeds of Excellence
  Choose from the best instead of the worst.

This Week's Tongue Tonics:
  • Echo and Inquire
  • Investigate Layers of Meaning
  • Definitive Descriptions
  • Drop Those Defenses
  • Salute!
  • Don't Deter Feedback

"You were taught, with regard to your former way of life, to put off your old self, which is being corrupted by its deceitful desires; to be made new in the attitude of your minds; and to put on the new self, created to be like God in true righteousness and holiness" (Eph. 4:22-24).

Cut out the Scripture card and post in a prominent place.

The Power of Exchange:
Out with the old—in with the new.
Psalms 39 and 40

This Talk Show guide will help you follow the video for Session Three.

1. Empty spaces beg to be _____.

When it comes to our hearts, it isn't enough to clean out the bad. We need to harness the power of exchange to intentionally fill up those empty spaces. Otherwise, our work of cleaning and weeding will have been for naught.

2. King David grew increasingly frustrated that he had nothing _____ to say to his adversaries.

To harness the power of exchange, David made some adjustments. David cried out, "Show me, O Lord." He changed four areas of his life.

a. Focus: from microscopic to _____ (see Ps. 39:4-7).

   Look at the big picture.

b. Mode of Operation: from autonomy to _____ on God (Ps. 39:8-12).

   Reliance is humble, teachable, and dependent on God.

c. Commitment: from impatience to _____ (see Ps. 39:13–40:2).

   Stick with it for the long haul.

d. Habit: from silence to _____ (see Ps. 40:8-10).

   God will give you something new to say–words of God's love.

The result: "Many will see and fear and put their trust in the Lord" (Ps. 40:3).

When we turn to God to help us transform the empty spaces in our hearts into welcoming, cultivated places, people will notice. Many will see and marvel and put their trust in the Lord. That's the power of exchange!

Seeds of Truth
Sow truth instead of falsehood.

"Then you will know the truth, and the truth will set you free." John 8:32

The chair was ugly and comfortable. I can't even remember where it came from, but that mismatched, olive-green, brocade chair was a definite eyesore. Even when it was covered with a creamy crocheted throw, I detested the sight of it. No one ever sat in it. Its sole purpose was to fill the huge empty space in the corner of our sparsely furnished family room.

One day I had had enough. I tossed the throw into the linen cupboard and triumphantly carted the chair out to the trash. Lopsided it sat, like a rejected friend, on top of the garbage cans. Day after day it remained there, the gaudy green peering out from under an eyebrow of fresh powdered snow.

It bothered me to see it there, but what bothered me even more was the gaping emptiness in the corner of the room. We did not have the resources to buy a new piece of furniture, and I had no idea how long that corner would remain empty. So just hours before the chair would have met its demise in the city dump, I found myself rescuing it. Muttering under my breath, I brushed the snow off, returned it to its original place, and retrieved its disguise from the linen closet.

Empty spaces beg to be filled. This principle applies to our hearts and our speech. Last week, through repentance, we cleaned out the ugly sin that was sitting in the corners of our hearts and mouths. In confessing and renouncing it, we triumphantly carted it out of our homes to the trash. But now there is an empty space where wrong attitudes, thoughts, and speech used to be.

The principle of exchange teaches us that our hearts must be filled with good things in order to keep the ugliness from moving back in. This week, we will sow seeds to plant new patterns of thought in our minds. The first seeds we will sow are seeds of truth.

Put Off the Old, Put On the New

Reread this week's Breath Freshener on page 50. What are we to do with the "old self" which is being corrupted with deceit? Underline it.

The verb *put off* means "to strip off, as in the case of filthy clothes." Paul reminded the Christians in Ephesus that when they became disciples of Jesus, they shed their old garments of deception.[1] Then they were "to put on the new self" (v. 24).

The word *new (kainos)* means entirely new in character—not merely renovated. The new self is new because it is created to be like God. The Greek means literally, "according to what God is." In challenging the Christians to put on the new, Paul told them to dress more and more like God. Putting off the old and putting on the new is an ongoing process of becoming more Christlike (sanctification).[1]

According to Paul, what part of the body needs to be dressed with the new? (see Eph. 4:23).

❑ arms   ❑ legs   ❑ mind   ❑ torso

Putting on the new means that we dress our minds with new clothing. Paul explains that this means replacing patterns of falsehood with patterns of truth (see Eph. 4:25). Later in the Book of Ephesians, he cites truth as the first of six essential pieces of clothing that soldiers must put on to gain victory in the battle of life.

"Sanctify them by the truth; your word is truth."
John 17:17

Read Ephesians 6:14. Circle the piece of soldier's clothing Paul associates with truth:

In Paul's time, the belt was an essential piece of military clothing. To prepare himself for combat, a soldier would cinch his tunic beneath his belt so it would not impede him as he charged into battle. The belt helped the soldier run and move about freely. Without a belt, a soldier would trip and fall.

How will truth help you? Match the benefit with the correct reference:

Truth will lead you into godliness.	Psalm 40:11
Truth will help you mature.	John 8:32
Truth will protect you.	Ephesians 4:15
Truth will set you free from sin.	Titus 1:1

Truth Defeats the Lies We Believe

Truth—the opposite of deceit—guards our hearts and minds from being misled. It purifies and keeps the soil of our hearts pure. That's why it is so important to make sure our thoughts are based on truth and that we sow seeds of truth in our hearts on an ongoing basis. Without truth, we trip and fall.

"We demolish arguments and every pretension [deceit] that sets itself up against the knowledge of God, and we take captive every thought to make it obedient to Christ."

2 Corinthians 10:5

Second Corinthians 10:5 says that taking our thoughts captive means tucking them firmly under the belt of truth. It means believing what God says and rejecting all other thoughts.

Every area of defeat and bondage in our lives can be traced back to the lies that we believe. Do you recognize any of the following lies? Put a check beside the lies you struggle with:

❏ God isn't good. **Truth:** He is good (see Ps. 119:68).

❏ God doesn't love me. **Truth:** He loves you (see Jer. 31:3; Rom. 8:38-39).

❏ I am unacceptable. **Truth:** In Christ, you are accepted (see Eph. 1:6).

❏ I am better/worse than others. **Truth:** We are all in need of God's grace and sanctification (see Rom. 3:10; 1 Thess. 5:23).

❏ God isn't concerned about me. **Truth:** He is concerned about every aspect of your life (see Matt. 10:30).

❏ I can't trust God to meet my needs. **Truth:** He will meet every need (see Phil. 4:19).

❏ God is not big enough to do it. **Truth:** He is all-powerful (see Jer. 32:17; Matt. 19:26; Phil. 3:21).

❏ I can't beat the sin in my life. **Truth:** God enables you to live righteously (see Rom. 6:6-7,22).

❏ I can't beat my past. **Truth:** He makes all things new (see 1 Cor. 6:11; 2 Cor. 5:17).

❏ I can't do what God says. **Truth:** He enables you to do everything He asks (see Phil. 4:13).

❏ I can't forgive. **Truth:** You can "forgive as the Lord forgave you" (Col. 3:13).

❏ I need to be in control. **Truth:** You can relinquish control to God (see Matt. 17:24-25; Gal. 2:20).

❏ I need to stand up for my own rights. **Truth:** The way of Christ is to give up rights (see Phil. 2:6-7).

❏ I need to pursue my own happiness. **Truth:** Happiness is found in pursuing God (see Matt. 5:6).

❏ I need to point out other people's sins. **Truth:** In humility I can regard others better than myself and consider their interests before my own (see Matt. 7:3; Phil. 2:3-4).

❏ If I don't fight back, I'll get walked on. **Truth:** I can turn the other cheek (see Matt. 5:39-42).

❏ I can discern other people's motives. **Truth:** Only God knows the heart (see 1 Chron. 28:9).

❏ I have a right to retaliate when hurt. **Truth:** Jesus says forgive (see Matt. 18:21-22).

❏ Other people make me sin. **Truth:** I alone am responsible for what I think, say, and do (see Ezek. 18:19-22; Rev. 20:13).

❏ Righteous people shouldn't suffer. **Truth:** Suffering is a tool that God uses to make us like Jesus (see Heb. 2:10; 1 Pet. 4:12-19).

❏ It's all about me. **Truth:** Everything is from Him, through Him, and to Him. It's all about God (see Rom. 11:36).[2]

Often we who have been given truth are trapped in defeat and bondage because we continue to believe lies. Take a moment right now to take captive your thoughts and bind them with truth. Ask God's Spirit–the Spirit of truth–to guide you (see John 14:16-17). Make this a habit. Every time you think a thought that is out of line with God's truth, ask Him to help you grab hold of that thought and put it back in place–under the belt of truth. Transformed speech is the result of a mind that is renewed with truth.

Reading and memorizing Scripture is the best way to buckle truth in place. Begin memorizing our weekly Breath Freshener today. On three- by-five-inch cards, write the verses of truth that correct the lies you identified. Hang them on your refrigerator, computer, mirror, or any other place where you will see them often.

Today's Tongue Tonic will teach you how to echo and inquire to ensure you understand what others are saying. When we listen, we want to discover a person's true feelings and motivation and not react based on our own false perceptions. Remember, our hearts can be deceitful. You can really improve your communication skills by learning and practicing the important skill of clarifying meaning.

Echo and Inquire

With every message there are potentials for miscommunication. Check to see if you have truly understood what the other person is trying to communicate before you respond. The two key techniques for checking are nondefensive *echo* and *inquire*.

ECHO: When we echo, we bounce back to others the messages they have conveyed to us through paraphrasing and resonating. *Paraphrasing* echoes back the verbal message by accurately and succinctly restating the message in your own words. *Resonating* reflects back the emotional part of the message. It reports our perception of what the speaker is feeling. Resonating can also report our perception of why he or she is feeling that way. "You feel … because… " In nondefensively offering the speaker our version of the message, we give him or her the opportunity to either confirm or correct our understanding.

INQUIRE: We can clarify meaning by asking questions. Direct and open-ended questions can give us valuable insight into what someone is thinking and feeling. *Direct questions* require a simple factual response. "Did you like that show?" Direct questions tend to be straightforward and precise in scope. They don't usually invite much elaboration from the speaker but can be helpful in asking for specific information. *Open-ended questions* offer the speaker more leeway to respond and share. They invite the speaker to expand or elaborate on her message: "What was the upsetting part for you about what I said?" "How did you feel when he told you he wouldn't do it?" Open-ended questions encourage others to "open up" and share their thoughts, feelings, and opinions.

Seeds of Abundance

Focus on what is received instead of what is owed.

"In him we have redemption through his blood, the forgiveness of sins, in accordance with the riches of God's grace, that he lavished on us."
Ephesians 1:7-8

In this week's Talk Show, we saw how David progressed from being empty to being filled with goodness. When David was focused on what he should have been receiving from the people who bothered him—respect and kindness, for example—he had nothing good to say. Yet when he became focused on his relationship to God and kept his focus there, he found himself filled with "a new song" and began to say good things to his adversaries. David teaches us an important principle:

> Our ability to give good to others springs from the abundance of good we receive from God.

Focus on Abundance

Imagine a girl with a few gummy bears. Her friend has a chocolate bar. The girl is reluctant to share her gummy bears unless she receives a piece of chocolate in return. She is focused on the scarcity of her candy. But if that girl had an abundance of gummy bears—a huge bagful in her hand, a barrelful in her room, and a father who promised to continually give her more—she would be much more likely to share freely. She would probably give away gummy bears all the time without demanding candy in return. For a small piece of chocolate, her friend might receive 10 pounds of gummy bears. Knowing she had plenty would encourage the girl to be generous.

A focus on scarcity results in stinginess while a focus on abundance results in generosity. If we focus on the resources of God, we realize we have an abundance to give. On the other hand, if we focus on what we should be getting from others, we become "stingy" and reluctant to give.

This principle extends to all areas of our lives, including our speech. We become increasingly patient the more we realize how patient God is with us. We love more when we realize how much God loves us. Our capacity to forgive increases as we become aware of how much God forgives us. We are gracious because we have been the recipients of so much grace. We are generous because of God's generosity. We are kind because God is kind to us. We are merciful because we receive mercy. When we focus on the overwhelming, abundant grace God has given and will continue to give to us, we are able to give abundantly to others.

According to Matthew 10:8, why were the disciples able to "freely give"?

_____

Match the following verses with your blessings from God:

Mercy	Romans 2:4
Love	Colossians 1:14
Kindness	Hebrews 4:16
Forgiveness	2 Peter 3:9
Patience	1 John 3:1

These are just a few of the many blessings God gives us. We don't deserve them, but He gives them to us anyway: "From the fullness of his grace we have all received one blessing after another" (John 1:16). He has "lavished" the "riches of [his] grace" upon us (Eph. 1:7-8).

Lavish means "an extravagant outpouring; bestowing in great abundance; exceedingly liberal; given with profusion." God has lavished us with one blessing after another–blessing upon blessing upon blessing from the fullness of His grace. We are impoverished beggars who have received a wealth of forgiveness, mercy, patience, love, and compassion. Our Heavenly Father has given us an inheritance of unimaginable proportions. Being stingy with what we have received is simply not an appropriate response.

"Heal the sick, raise the dead, cleanse those who have leprosy, drive out demons. Freely you have received, freely give."
Matthew 10:8

Practice the Principle of Exchange

In Jesus' parable told in Matthew 18:21-35, the master forgave the servant an enormous debt. However, the servant was unable to forgive his fellow servant who owed him just a few dollars. In demanding payment for the small debt, the unforgiving servant demonstrated disregard for the mercy that had been shown to him. That's why the master revoked his gift and demanded full payment.

This parable illustrates our relationship to God. God has been immeasurably gracious to us. He has forgiven us a debt that we could never pay. He continues to pour grace upon us every moment of every day. Because we receive so much from God, it is natural and right for us to cancel the comparably small debts our fellow humans owe us. His abundance of forgiveness is our source of abundance.

When we reach the end of our hoarded resources, Our Father's full giving is only begun. His love has no limit, His grace has no measure, His power no boundary known unto men; For out of His infinite riches in Jesus He giveth and giveth and giveth again.
—Annie Johnson Flint

Answer the questions by reading the verses in parentheses:

1. Why should we be patient and forgive the grievances that we have against others (see Col. 3:13)?

_____

2. Why should we show mercy to those who don't deserve it (see Luke 6:36)?

_____

If people do or say something to hurt us, we feel we are owed an apology. In our minds, they owe us a debt. Kindness, patience, respect, understanding, politeness, or even silence is what we expected. But because they didn't "pay" these things, our balance books record a withdrawal on their account.

Imagine that you are at a social gathering. A friend approaches you and says something sarcastic, belittling you in front of others. You feel humiliated and shamed.

On the stack of coins below on the left, mark off how much you feel that person "owes" you.

Totally indebted—owing everything up to and including life itself

Not owing anything

On the stack of coins above on the right, mark off how much you owe God for that which He has freely forgiven you.

If we feel someone owes us, we may be tempted to "balance the books" of that person's debt. We do this by replying with an equally cutting remark, by thinking bad thoughts, by slandering–speaking behind his/her back, by harboring resentment and bitterness, or getting back in some other way.

Was your mark right at the top of the stack of coins? Compare what the person owes you to what you would owe God were it not for His grace. According to Christ's parable, the enormity of forgiveness that I receive from God requires that I release others from the debt they owe me. The principle of exchange requires that I base my words on the transaction that has occurred between the Lord and me–not between me and another person. It means that I focus on God's abundance and not on what others owe. The belief that I must balance the books when others hurt me is based on deceit. It neglects the gift of grace I receive from God and denies the value of His gift.

The abundance of what He gives empowers you to sow seeds of abundance. And seeds of abundance will lead to an abundant harvest. Freely you have received–freely give.

Investigate Layers of Meaning

Each message contains layers of meaning. Asking, "What do you mean?" can be helpful, but often, we receive better information when we ask more specific questions. Four questions investigate the manifest meaning, while the other four investigate the implicit meaning.

Manifest Meaning

DETAILS: Ask who, what, when, where, how, and why. Here's a tip: Try to use "what" instead of "why" questions. They sound less interrogating. For example, instead of asking, "Why didn't you call me?" ask, "What kept you from calling me?"

DEFINITIONS: Ask questions to clarify particular words in the message. When your spouse says, "You always favor your side of the family!" you could ask, "What do you mean by *favor*"? Alternately, you could put forth your own definition to see if his is the same: "When you say *favor* do you mean that I spend more time with them?"

DEGREE: When someone makes a generalization, ask questions to clarify the amount of time and/or quantity that person has in mind. In response to the previous statement, you could ask your spouse, "Do you think I favor them all the time–or just at Christmas?"

DIARY: Ask questions to understand the other person's emotions, beliefs and actions, or motivations–items they might record in their diary. You might ask your spouse, "Do you believe that spending more time with my side of the family at Christmas indicates that we love them more than yours?"

Implicit Meaning

OBSERVABLE REACTIONS: Ask questions about reactions you observe. "I notice your furrowed brow. What are you thinking?" "That was a heavy sigh. What are you feeling?"

INTERPRETATION: Ask for their interpretation of your words and behavior. "Do you think I sounded judgmental when I shared my opinion with you?" "Do you think I react defensively when your mother comes over?"

ATTITUDE OR EMOTION: Ask questions to understand the person's attitude (skepticism, hostility, sarcasm, superiority) or emotion (hurt, irritation, impatience).

MOTIVATION AND INTENTIONS: Ask what is causing a person to react a certain way or what he is seeking to accomplish. "Are you upset because I was late today, or is there more behind the way you are feeling?" "How are you wanting me to respond?

Seeds of Grace

Be a grace-giver instead of a debt-counter.

"Let us then approach the throne of grace with confidence, so that we may receive mercy and find grace to help us in our time of need."
Hebrews 4:16

We have a black Labrador named Beauregard. When we first brought him home, we were amazed by the size of his coat—at least four sizes too big for his body. When I pulled up the skin at the scruff of his neck, there was so much there it seemed another dog could fit inside. His body was comically small in proportion to his wrapping. Like Beau, I am comically small in proportion to the coat of grace with which God has clothed me. His grace is so big and magnificent that I feel small, inadequate, and incapable of filling it out. Quoting Augustine I say, "What is grace? I know until you ask me; when you ask me, I do not know."

Augustine knew enough about God's grace to realize that he knew very little of it. So little, in fact, that in a sense he knew nothing of it at all. The grace of God is so enormous, so wonderful, so attractive, so exceedingly great and abundant that our minds cannot even begin to comprehend it, and our words cannot even begin to describe it.

Yesterday, we learned that it is from God's abundance that we have an abundance to give to others. Today we will we see that the source of this abundance is God's grace (see John 1:16). Grace elects (see Rom. 11:5), calls (see Gal. 1:15), and justifies us (see Rom. 3:24). Through grace, God produces faith in our hearts (see Acts 15:11), forgives our sins (see Eph. 1:7), saves us (see Eph. 2:5,8), consoles us and gives us hope (see 2 Thess. 2:16). We are freed by grace (see Rom. 6:14), given gifts of grace (see 2 Cor. 9:8-9), and are heirs of future grace (see 1 Pet. 3:7).

Grace is the central lynchpin of all we are, all we have, and all we will be in Christ. God's grace got us where we are, helps us where we are, and gives us hope for where we are going. The Bible says that grace ought to fill and transform our speech (see Col. 4:6). So for the purpose of this study, let's explore the word *grace*.

Transformed speech results from a mind renewed with the truth revealed through Jesus, a heart profoundly grateful for God's abundant grace, and a resolve to work at planting seeds that will grow into a harvest of righteousness.

The title of a book made the statement, "Grace is not a blue-eyed blonde." Define *grace* in your own words.

Read today's Word from the Word to understand more about the meaning of the word *grace*.

[grace] An Unmerited Gift

The Greek word for *grace* is *charis* from which we derive the word *charity*. The grace of God is the unmerited love and favor of God towards humanity. We do not deserve His grace. There is nothing we can ever do to earn His grace. And we can never hope to repay Him for His grace.

"God of all grace" is one of God's names (1 Pet. 5:10). He is the source and giver of all grace. His grace is full (see John 1:16), "glorious" (Eph. 1:6), rich (see Eph. 2:7), "abundant" (Rom. 5:17), exceeding, abounding (see 2 Cor. 9:14), overflowing (see Rom. 5:15), "sufficient" (2 Cor. 12:9), and "indescribable" (2 Cor. 9:15).

God's greatest expression of grace is the free gift of salvation offered through His Son, Jesus (see Rom. 5:15). His grace pays our debt, lavishes "one blessing after another" upon us (John 1:16), and promises us an unimaginably generous outpouring of God's favor in the future (see 1 Pet. 1:13). No wonder the writer of the well-known hymn exclaimed, "Amazing Grace!"

The favorable disposition God has toward you enables you to have a favorable disposition toward others. We have a natural tendency to be debt-counters–keeping track when others fail and paying them back or expecting them to pay up. But God's grace counteracts this tendency. With His grace, we can look with favor on those who least deserve those things from us. We can–like Him–be grace-givers.

How do you feel about the last statement, "We can–like Him– be grace-givers"? (Check one.)
❑ Uninterested–I'd rather bear a grudge.
❑ Intimidated–there's no way I can do it!
❑ Unsure–what will it cost?
❑ Eager–may it be so!

Actions Accompany Grace

A disposition of grace is always accompanied by actions of grace. The Father demonstrated His grace by sending His Son, Jesus Christ. Jesus demonstrated His grace when He became flesh, dwelt among humanity, died to bear the penalty of our sin, and rose victoriously to secure our future hope (see Rom. 5). The amazing grace of God is also demonstrated on an ongoing basis as He pours one blessing after another out upon us (see John 1:16).

It was evident by Christ's actions that He was "full of grace and truth" (John 1:14). Not only was grace evident in what Christ did, but also it was evident in what He said. The grace on the inside spilled over into His words.

"Grow in the grace and knowledge of our Lord and Savior Jesus Christ. To him be glory both now and forever!"
2 Peter 3:18

Read Luke 4:22. What amazed people about Jesus?

Psalm 45 prophesies the coming of Christ. How was Jesus uniquely prepared to be God's ambassador (see v. 2)?
❑ He was briefed on what the Jews expected.
❑ His lips were anointed with grace.
❑ His tongue was seasoned with truth.
❑ His mouth was filled with righteousness.

Anointing signified an appointment to a special place or function in the purpose of God. God anointed Christ's lips with grace because Christ was going to express God's message of grace to His objects of grace: sinful, undeserving humans.

In receiving God's amazing grace, humans also receive the capacity to become like Him. As E. Stanley Jones so aptly said, once we grab onto the gift of grace we are "bound to catch the spirit of the Giver. Like produces like."[3] In our actions and in our speech, we become more and more like God.

"Grace binds you with far stronger cords than the cords of duty or obligation can bind you. Grace is free, but when once you take it you are bound forever to the Giver, and bound to catch the spirit of the Giver. Like produces like. Grace makes you gracious, the Giver makes you give."[3]
—E. Stanley Jones

Grace affects our conduct. As recipients of grace we begin to do good works (see Eph. 2:8-10) and work hard at giving grace to others (see 1 Cor. 15:10). This is not because we *owe* God or could ever hope to pay Him back. No. Grace is free. We owe nothing. Yet our conduct changes as a result of being filled. We become like the One who pours His grace into us. As His abundant grace fills us, it begins to define who we are, and of necessity—reflex action, really—it affects what we do.

Grace Affects Our Speech

In Colossians 4:6, to what are gracious words compared? Circle the correct picture.

In biblical times, salt was used as a seasoning and preservative to add flavor to food and to keep it from spoiling. In rabbinical literature, salt is used metaphorically as a symbol of wisdom.[4] Salt was included in Old Testament grain offerings as a symbol of friendship and communion with God (see Lev. 2:13). The idea Paul communicated in Colossians is that just as salt seasons and preserves food, gracious, wise words season and preserve our relationships.

God's grace enables our speech to be gracious by our

- being humble, considering the perspective of others, and respecting their strengths (see Rom. 12:3-8);
- being authentic, showing others who we really are (see 1 Cor. 15:9-10);
- having an attitude of service and gratitude (see 2 Cor. 4:5-15);
- being wise in how we speak (see Col. 4:6);
- conducting ourselves with holiness and sincerity (see 2 Cor. 1:12).

If God's grace changes our speech so dramatically, why do Christians still struggle with their mouths? The Bible explains that it is possible to "receive God's grace in vain" (2 Cor. 6:1) or to miss it (see Heb. 12:15). How do we appropriate the grace of God? The answer is found in Hebrews 4:16.

We can boldly approach God and ask for His grace for our every need. His grace will fill and transform us and change us from a debt-counter into a grace-giver. Transformed speech is speech overflowing with God's grace.

Today's Tongue Tonic shows how you can have the grace to verify your perceptions and refrain from jumping to conclusions.

"Let us then approach the throne of grace with confidence, so that we may receive mercy and find grace to help us in our time of need." Hebrews 4:16

Verify Decoding

Problems arise when we don't verify the way we have decoded someone else's behavior and then jump to conclusions about what they are thinking and feeling. Our interpretations are often wrong. That's why it is so important to verify decoding by using a **DART**:

DESCRIBE BEHAVIOR: Describe the verbal, vocal, and visual behavior you observe. ("I notice that you ..." "You are ...")

ADVANCE ALTERNATIVES: Offer some alternate interpretations of the behavior. ("I wonder if ..." "Could it be that ...")

REQUEST CLARIFICATION: Ask for clarification about how to interpret the behavior. ("How do you feel?" "What do you think?")

TEST AND TRANSMIT: Test your current decoding, correct it, and transmit your new understanding. ("So you think that ..." "You feel ...") Use another DART if necessary.

In order for your DART to be effective, self-check that the vocal (calm, relaxed voice) and visual (SALUTE, see p. 71) parts of your message also communicate non-defensiveness. These shouldn't be sharp. They are for clarifying, not for attacking!

63

Day Four

Seeds of Gratitude
Be thankful instead of unthankful.

"Therefore, since we are receiving a kingdom that cannot be shaken, let us be thankful, and so worship God acceptably with reverence and awe."
Hebrews 12:28

One of the first phrases I taught my children was *thank you*. This concept went far beyond speech manners. They learned that receiving is a privilege, not a right. Good things are something for which to be humbly grateful rather than something to expect and demand.

As 1 Corinthians 4:7 asks: "What do you have that you did not receive? And if you did receive it, why do you boast as though you did not?" Just consider this: our lives, our health, our gifts and abilities, our possessions—we have nothing that we did not receive.

The Fruit of Our Lips

Read the following verses describing the ungodly.

People will be lovers of themselves, lovers of money, boastful, proud, abusive, disobedient to their parents, ungrateful, unholy, without love, unforgiving, slanderous, without self-control, brutal, not lovers of the good, treacherous, rash, conceited, lovers of pleasure rather than lovers of God (2 Tim. 3:2-4).

Did you realize that ungratefulness is a sign of ungodliness? The more inclined we are towards God, the more grateful and less arrogant we will be. God's grace humbles us, makes our lips overflow with thanksgiving, and in turn, affects the way we speak to others.

[thanks] An Overflow of Grace

Charis is a Greek word for *thanks*. It has the same root that is translated "grace." *Charis* means a disposition of kindness, favor, and grace on the part of the giver and thanks, respect, and homage on the part of the receiver.

Conceptually, the two go hand in hand. God's *charis* flowing into us causes us to overflow with *charis*. As a result, we become characterized by a disposition that is kind and gracious. That is why we are able to give thanks for everything (see Eph. 5:20), "everyone" (1 Tim. 2:1), and "in all circumstances" (1 Thess. 5:18).

A "chari-table" disposition naturally overflows from the *charis* we receive from God. His grace toward us fills us up so that we can overflow with grace toward those around us.

Read Hebrews 13:15-16. What are we to continually offer to God as a sacrifice of thanksgiving?

❏ a perfect lamb ❏ turtledoves
❏ fruit of our lips ❏ pot roast

"Through Jesus, therefore, let us continually offer to God a sacrifice of praise–the fruit of lips that confess his name. And do not forget to do good and to share with others, for with such sacrifices God is pleased." Hebrews 13:15-16

According to Old Testament Law (see Lev. 1–7), Jews were obliged to follow a system of offering sacrifices to the Lord. There were numerous types of sacrifices: lambs, bulls, goats, rams, turtledoves, pigeons, flour, grain, oil-baked cakes, and frankincense.

The sacrifices were offered for various reasons. Sin and trespass sacrifices were offered as atonement for sin. Whole burnt offerings were an expression of complete dedication and consecration to God. Peace offerings symbolized fellowship with God. Grain offerings expressed gratitude. Sin and trespass offerings were compulsory, but whole burnt offerings as well as peace and grain offerings were voluntary.

The Book of Hebrews explains that the blood of Christ, offered for our sins, canceled the need for sin and trespass offerings (see Heb. 9–10). Under the "new covenant" that God made with humanity (Heb. 9:15), Jesus' sacrifice paid for all our failures. Consequently, through His grace, we owe God nothing. The obligation has been met. Our debt has been paid in full.

The Book of Hebrews speaks of the sufficiency of Christ's sacrifice to pay our debt. Why then does the writer conclude his letter by encouraging readers to

 … An humble mind is the soil out of which thanks naturally grow.—A proud man is seldom a grateful man, for he never thinks he gets as much as he deserves. —Henry Ward Beecher

offer sacrifices? The answer lies in the type of sacrifice he encourages us to give: a sacrifice of thanks from the fruit of our lips.

Fruit indicates that this type of sacrifice is like the Old Testament grain offering which was a voluntary, not obligatory, gift to God. The absence of leaven (yeast) symbolized the absence of sin and the presence of sincerity and truth (see 1 Cor. 5:6-9).

Therefore, what the writer of Hebrews seems to be implying with his imagery is this: gratitude to God is expressed in lips that praise Him, but it is also expressed by the absence of sin and the presence of sincerity and truth in our speech.

A heart filled with the Holy Spirit results in lips that confess the name of Jesus. The fruit of our lips–God-praising, gracious, thankful, pure, sincere speech–demonstrates our heart's allegiance to Him.

Read 1 Peter 2:1-5. What do those who are part of God's house of holy priests do (see v. 5)? Write your answer in the margin.

Under the Old Covenant, only the priests entered the most holy place of the presence of God to offer sacrifices. Because of Christ's sacrifice, all believers are now "priests" able to stand in His presence (1 Pet. 2:9). We do not need to offer up the obligatory sacrifice for sin. Through Christ, that has been done once and for all. But we do have the privilege of offering up voluntary spiritual sacrifices that demonstrate our dedication, consecration, fellowship, and gratitude to God.

First Peter 2:1-2 cites two characteristics of those who offer spiritual sacrifices. Fill in the missing information.

Those offering spiritual sacrifices rid themselves of (see v. 1):

_____

_____ .

They crave (see v. 2): _____

The Fruit of Our Actions

"Among you there must not be even a hint of sexual immorality, or any kind of impurity, or of greed, because these are improper for God's holy people. Nor should there be any obscenities, foolish talk or coarse joking, which are out of place, but rather thanksgiving."
Ephesians 5:3-4

Humble gratefulness is the appropriate response to the grace of God. Ephesians 5:3-4 demonstrates how our gratitude shows up in our attitudes, actions, and words toward others.

• Holy actions are practiced and unholy ones renounced (those that are immoral, impure, and selfish).
• Words of thankfulness are spoken instead of obscene and foolish words or coarse joking.

We are often encouraged to "be positive," "look on the bright side," or to realize that "every cloud has silver lining." However, being thankful for difficult people and in difficult circumstances is not based on psyching ourselves up to have a good attitude. Instead, our gratitude must flow from a more reliable source.

In 2 Corinthians 4:13-18, Paul said the source of our gratitude is "faith in the grace of God." In faith we believe and speak because we know that the Father has poured, is pouring, and will continue to pour out His grace on us. Because of that we will receive eternal glory. It is His grace that causes "thanksgiving to overflow to the glory of God" (v. 15).

Thanksgiving overflows so that whatever you do whether in word or deed, you are able to "do it all in the name of the Lord Jesus giving thanks to God the Father through him" (Col. 3:17).

Transformed speech flows from a heart that is profoundly grateful for His grace. Close today's lesson by expressing your gratitude for God's grace poured out on you through Jesus. Ask Him to make your thanksgiving flow over into your words and deeds.

In today's Tongue Tonic you will learn to be more definitive in your descriptions and to drop your defenses toward others.

Definitive Descriptions

When giving feedback, it's helpful to describe to the other person what it was that led to our interpretation. The more precise we can be in expressing what we have observed, the greater our chance of clearly communicating our perspective.

Problems occur when we mix interpretations into our descriptions. To avoid this tendency, we should aim to make our descriptions specific rather than general, concrete rather than abstract, situational rather than global, objective rather than subjective, and descriptive rather than interpretive. Definitive descriptions increase clarity, decrease the hearer's defensiveness, and increase the likelihood of the situation being addressed in a constructive manner. In the following interaction, notice the difference a definitive description makes.

Less Definitive	**More Definitive**
"You don't care about me."	"You forgot an important occasion."
"You don't want to do your share."	"You rolled your eyes, shook your head, sighed, and threw the paper down when I asked you to help. I assume you are reluctant to help me."

Drop Those Defenses

Many verbal, vocal, and visual behaviors can convey that we are not open and receptive. To send the right message, we must avoid the following defensive behaviors.

VERBAL: *Superlatives*–"You always ..." "It's only ... "
Negative Contractions–"Haven't you finished yet?" conveys a very different message than "Have you finished?"
Weighted Words–"Really," "just," "still," "yet" imply disbelief, disapproval, or defensiveness. "Do you really ... ?" "Are you still ... ?"
Frame/Box/Bias–Our presuppositions can present themselves as defensive verbal behavior when we use state of being verbs and generalizations to present personal opinions as facts. For example, saying, "That's ridiculous!"

VOCAL: Emphasizing the last word of a statement or raising pitch at the end of a question tends to give the message a tone of increased emotion, urgency, and expectation. To be non-defensive, your voice should remain calm and even; vocal pitch should remain neutral or drop slightly at the end of statements and questions.

VISUAL: *Body indicators* such as pushing head and neck forward, tilting head to side (can appear condescending), shaking head in disagreement, shrugging shoulders (indicating unimportance). *Facial indicators* such as frowning, squinting, smirking, opening eyes wide, raising eyebrows, wrinkling forehead, pursing lips.

Day Five

Seeds of Excellence

Choose from the best instead of the worst.

"Now he who supplies seed to the sower and bread for food will also supply and increase your store of seed and will enlarge the harvest of your righteousness."
2 Corinthians 9:10

Have you ever worked one of those connect-the-dot puzzles? Looking at the puzzle, you can see all the various points, but the picture isn't revealed until you connect them with lines. This week's lessons connect to present a picture of how we can harness the power of exchange. Exchange is essentially the process of putting new things into our lives so we become more and more like Jesus.

Two main attributes of Jesus are grace and truth. The Bible says: "The Word became flesh and made his dwelling among us. We have seen his glory, the glory of the One and Only, who came from the Father, full of grace and truth" (John 1:14). Grace and truth are foundational to Christ's character and to our transformation. Our speech will increase in godliness as we increase in grace and truth.

We began this week by discussing the need for a mind renewed with truth. In the following lessons, we saw that gracious speech flows from a heart overwhelmed by God's grace. In today's lesson we will learn how to choose and plant the seeds that lead to a bountiful harvest. The following summary statement connects the dots between all the concepts:

> Transformed speech results from a mind renewed with the truth revealed through Jesus, a heart profoundly grateful for God's abundant grace, and a resolve to work at planting seeds that will grow into a harvest of righteousness.

To harness the power of exchange, we need what?

1. A mind renewed with t_____.

2. A heart profoundly grateful for God's g_____.

3. A resolve to w_____at planting seeds.

Sow Generously

Read the following passage from 2 Corinthians:

> *Remember this: Whoever sows sparingly will also reap sparingly, and whoever sows generously will also reap generously. And God is able to make all grace abound to you, so that in all things at all times, having all that you need, you will abound*

in every good work. Now he who supplies seed to the sower and bread for food will also supply and increase your store of seed and will enlarge the harvest of your righteousness. You will be made rich in every way so that you can be generous on every occasion, and through us your generosity will result in thanksgiving to God (vv. 9:6,8,10-11).

This passage refers to the specific situation of the Corinthian Christians giving generously to meet the financial needs of others. However, the phrase *so that in all things at all times, having all that you need, you will abound in every good work* (v. 8) indicates that it is a principle that can be applied to other areas of our lives.

If we sow excellent seeds into our hearts, we will reap a harvest of excellence from our lips. The more generously we sow, the more generously we will reap.

In 2 Corinthians 9:10, from where does the seed we sow for good works come?
❑ last year's harvest
❑ the grocery store
❑ a small paper packet
❑ the supplier

What has the supplier of seed promised to do?

_____

The one who supplied the seed also supplies and enlarges our store of seeds, enlarges the harvest, and makes us rich.

What are we expected to do? Write true (T) or false (F).

_____ We are expected to pay for the seed.

_____ We are expected to plant the seed.

_____ We are expected to bake the bread.

_____ We are expected to store the bread until Christmas.

_____ We are expected to be generous on every occasion.

Our job is quite simple. All we have to do is plant the seed that God provides and be generous with the harvest that He increases. The seed is to be drawn from the store that God provides.

Every thought is a seed. If you plant crabapples don't count on harvesting Golden Delicious.
—Author Unknown

69

The P-48 Test

How can we make sure we are sowing God's seed and not other seed? The Bible provides a filter we can use to judge whether or not the seed is from Him. I call it the P-48 test.

P-48 is based on Philippians 4:8. It tests the goodness of thoughts, beliefs, and words, so we can judge if they ought to be planted in our hearts. With P-48, we determine whether the seeds are:

Pure, **R**ight, **E**xcellent, **P**raiseworthy, **L**ovely, **A**dmirable, **N**oble, **T**rue

After being shaken through this filter, the words that remain are seeds we want to PRE-PLANT. The others are not from God and should be discarded. Put your thoughts and words to the test below:

Pure	Are my motives pure? Are my thoughts/words holy?
Right	Is this proper and appropriate? Is it in conformity with God's standards and principles? Does it build?
Excellent	Is this of highest quality? Is it the best or just adequate?
Praiseworthy	Is it commendable? Am I proud of the way I am thinking/speaking? Is God proud of me?
Lovely	Does it have a beauty that appeals to the heart? Does it mirror the beauty and gentleness of Jesus?
Admirable	Is it worthy of being respected and admired? Would others commend it?
Noble	Is it of the highest moral character, superior quality, great, and magnificent? Does it demonstrate my position as a child of the King?
True	Is it free of deceit? Does it agree with the Bible's evaluation of the situation? Does it submit to truth?

Memorize the P-48 acrostic. Apply this test to your thoughts and words. Ask God to help you filter out anything that does not meet this standard.

Read Colossians 3:5-17. Complete this chart with examples:

Things We Throw Out	Things We Plant

Establishing new ways of thinking and speaking is an ongoing process of exchange. It means throwing out what does not belong and actively planting what does.

By renewing your mind with truth, being profoundly grateful for His grace, and resolving to plant seeds of excellence, you will harness the power of exchange and experience more conversation peace.

[1]Peter T. O'Brien, *Word Biblical Commentary: Ephesians,* David A. Hubbard, Glenn W. Barker, eds., (Waco, TX: Word Publishing, 1987), 329-330.
[2]For more about this topic, contact Life Action Ministries by mail at P.O. Box 31, Buchanan, MI 49107-0031; by phone at 1-800-321-1538; by email at www.lifeaction.org, and request the video "Lies Women Believe and the Truth That Sets Them Free" by Nancy Leigh DeMoss.
[3]E. Stanley Jones, *The Way* (Nashville: Abingdon Press, 1946), 196.
[4]Peter T. O'Brien, *Word Biblical Commentary: Colossians, Philemon,* David A. Hubbard, Glenn W. Barker, eds., (Waco, TX: Word Publishing, 1987), 243.

Salute!

Actions speak louder than words. The way you position your body tells others how available you are to interact and how interested you are in what they have to say. If you want to signal others that you are relaxed, comfortable, open, and interested in them, then "salute" them with your body language. To salute is "to address with expressions of kind wishes."

SMILE: Wearing a warm smile is like hanging out a welcome sign. It invites people to relate to you.

AFFIRM: Affirm the speaker by nodding and affirmative vocal sounds. If you don't affirm the speaker in this way, she will probably assume that you disagree with her or are disinterested in what she has to say.

LEAN TOWARD: Leaning toward someone indicates your desire to engage with him or her–but lean only slightly. Leaning too far can indicate aggression.

UNLOCK POSTURE: Crossing your arms, closing your hands, holding your arms across your chest, clasping your hands together, or crossing your legs away from the other person are closed positions. They signal that you are defensive, guarded, or closed to interacting. Unlock your posture to communicate openness.

TOUCH: This expresses caring. If you want to show someone warmth, put your left hand on top of her right hand while shaking hands, touch her arm, pat her back, or give her a hug. The physical contact signals you are open to emotional contact.

EYE CONTACT: Eye contact is a powerful sign of respect and attention. It communicates, "Right now, I am more interested in you than anything else!" While conversing, make eye contact for one to ten seconds at a time, more while listening than while talking.

Don't Deter Feedback

Feedback from others is a valuable tool to help us understand them and to help us understand how our messages are being interpreted. We deter feedback when we immediately **deny it** ("That's not true"), **defend ourselves** ("That's because …"), **discount it** ("That's not a big deal ..."), or **disintegrate upon receiving it** ("I'm so hurt you think that …"). Listening to and understanding feedback is not the same thing as agreeing with it. Feedback provides useful information even when we differ with its content. Welcome it with listening ears. Don't Deter Feedback!

The Power of the Open Gate

Humility opens the door to effective communication.

Week Four

The Bible refers to the mouth as a gate: Our words can either shut people out or invite them in. Transformed speech lowers the drawbridge, raises the bars, and throws open the doors of our castles to unleash the power of the open gate.

Gates are highly significant structures. To understand their significance and how they relate to communication, this week's Talk Show will examine the story of the Tower of Babel, which in Hebrew means "gate of the gods."

Day 1: The High Gate of Battle
   ... *is opened with the key of peace.*
Day 2: The High Gate of Control
   ... *is opened with the key of relinquishment.*
Day 3: The High Gate of Assumption
   ... *is opened with the key of understanding.*
Day 4: The High Gate of Haste
   ... *is opened with the key of patience.*
Day 5: The High Gate of Entitlement
   ... *is opened with the key of self-sacrifice.*

This Week's Tongue Tonics:
- Three Tools of the Trade
- The Question: A Quest for Information
- Counterfeit Questions
- Making a Statement
- The Threefold RAP Statement
- Forecast: Your Statement of Intent
- Tools Instead of Weapons

"He who loves a quarrel loves sin; he who builds a high gate invites destruction" (Prov. 17:19).

Cut out the Scripture card on page 147 as a reminder for the week.

The Power of the Open Gate: Toppling the tongue tower
Genesis 11:1-11

This Talk Show guide will help you follow the video for Session Four.

1. Characteristics of Tongue Towers

a. Tongue Towers are _____ places–"above others."

b. Tongue Towers function as _____.
They represent power because they control access.

c. Tongue Towers create barriers to _____.
The people were talking but they weren't connecting.

2. Causes of Tongue Towers–Tongue Towers are built through prideful attitudes.

Attitude	Indicator	Motivator
Complacent	"settled there"	desire for ease/comfort
Independent	"let us"	desire for control
Self-centered	"for ourselves"	desire for gain
Striving	"bricks, bake, build city"	desire for acceptance
Self-promoting	"make a name"	desire for recognition
Fearful/defensive	"tower, not to be scattered"	desire for security
Presumptuous	"to the heavens"	desire for preeminence

3. Consequences of Tongue Towers

a. Their _____ was confused.

b. They were unable to _____ together.

c. They were _____–fractured relationships.

d. They experienced on-going pain and _____.

4. Counteracting Tongue Towers

Counteract with an _____ gate. Watch the high tower _____.

I open my gate when I have the right posture before God and the right perspective of God. Bowing in humility allows God's glory to flood into my life and into my words so I can experience the power of the open gate.

The High Gate of Battle
... is opened with the key of peace.

"The peace of God, which transcends all understanding, will guard your hearts and your minds in Christ Jesus."
Philippians 4:7

I know a young woman who is spending time in prison for killing her roommate. How did it happen? A quarrel got out of control. The verbal battle was intense, and when her roommate, who was taller and stronger, lunged at her with fists swinging, the girl grabbed the knife on the kitchen counter in self-defense. One girl died, and the other's life is forever damaged because of that moment of battle.

Proverbs 17:19, our Breath Freshener for the week, likens quarreling to putting up a high gate that invites destruction. When an enemy encounters a high gate, he will ram it, storm it, or try to set it on fire. In contrast to the open gate in times of peace, a high gate expects–and even invites–the conflict and siege of war to begin.

This week we will be examining some high gates that we erect with our mouths. The first high gate is the gate of battle. Most of us will never reach a point of physical blows and manslaughter, as those two girls did, but if we are honest, we must admit that our words have at times resulted in wounds that are equally tragic.

Our Battle Tactics

In our second week of lessons, we discussed how the tongue could be used as a sword or plow. The high gate of battle means that we enter conversations with our swords drawn. Even if we do not strike, we assume a posture to defend or attack.

Look over the following list of offensive and defensive battle tactics. Check the ones that you use:

Offensive: ATTACK
- ❑ accusing (see Prov. 3:30)
- ❑ harsh (see Prov. 15:1)
- ❑ hot-tempered (see Prov. 15:18)
- ❑ malicious (see Prov. 17:4)
- ❑ quarreling (see Prov. 20:3)
- ❑ ill-tempered (see Prov 25:24)
- ❑ mocking, scoffing (see Prov. 29:8)
- ❑ spouting off (Prov. 9:13)
- ❑ violent, abusive speech (see Prov. 10:11)
- ❑ unrestrained, out of control (see Prov. 17:27)
- ❑ destructive (see Prov. 11:9; 12:18)
- ❑ deceitful (see Prov 15:4; 17:20)
- ❑ scorching (see Prov. 16:27)
- ❑ arrogant (see Prov. 17:7)
- ❑ insulting (see Prov. 22:10)
- ❑ sarcastic (Prov. 26:18-19)
- ❑ angry (see Prov. 29:11)

Defensive: RETREAT

❑ fear (see Prov. 10:24; 29:25)
❑ evil thoughts (see Prov. 15:26)
❑ gloating (see Prov. 24:17-18)
❑ concealing hatred (see Prov. 10:12,18)
❑ lying, hiding feelings (see Prov. 12:17; 19:22)
❑ desiring revenge (see Prov. 13:2; 24:28-29)
❑ gossiping, slandering (see Prov. 16:28)
❑ independent spirit (see Prov. 21:24; 26:12)

❑ mocking inwardly (see Prov. 24:9)
❑ wounded spirit (see Prov. 26:6; Ps. 38:17-19)
❑ stirring up anger in spirit (see Prov. 30:33)
❑ hidden desires and envy (see Jas. 4:1)
❑ resentment (see Prov. 14:10)
❑ assuming (see Prov. 18:13)
❑ heavy spirit (see Prov. 27:3)

How many boxes did you check? Most of us struggle with the high gate of battle. We bar our gates, fortify our defenses, attack, and do battle–even with those we love the most. Proverbs 18:19 describes the unfortunate consequences of doing so:
  • hurt and wounded spirits
  • broken relationships
  • increased resistance, barriers
  • loss of intimacy (separation and distance)
  • stand-offs, entrenched situations
  • closed doors, each says to the other–"I won't let you in!"

Why do we battle? List reasons in the margin. Be prepared to share your reasons with the group.

The Source of Our Battle Posture

Read James 4:1-3. What causes fights and quarrels?
❑ when we don't get something we want
❑ when we can't have what we want
❑ when we envy those who have what we want
❑ when we look to people instead of God for what we want
❑ when we regard our own pleasure as the highest goal

All of these responses cause us to put up a gate of battle. Solomon summarized the problem in one word: *pride* (see Prov. 13:10). My definition for *pride* is "focusing on my own rights, ability, or insufficiency instead of on God's glory, grace, and all-sufficiency."

Pride also shows up in in insecurity. When we are wrapped up in self-concern, trying to meet our own desires or demanding that others meet them, pride is at work. Pride causes us to assume a battle posture.

Drop thy still dews of quietness till all our striving cease; Take from our souls the strain and stress, And let our ordered lives confess The beauty of thy Peace.
—John Greenleaf Whittier

Demolishing the Gate of Battle

How do we bring down the proud gate of battle? We must—in wisdom and humility—cultivate a spirit of peace.

Read James 3:13-18. A peacemaker who sows in peace has the opposite mind-set than someone who does battle. Describe the mind-set that characterizes a peacemaker (see v. 17).

_____

_____

_____

_____

"Blessed are the peacemakers, for they will be called sons of God." Matthew 5:9

Peace brings down barriers and destroys dividing walls of hostility. With God's peace we can have a tranquil spirit that is neither defensive nor combative. We can approach situations with plow in hand. Our attitude is not, "How can I get what I want?" but rather, "How can I till this soil? How can I cultivate this relationship? How do I honor God?" I can rest in the confidence that God will look after me. Read Word from the Word to find out more about biblical peace.

[peace] Bringing Down the Barrier

Peace is the absence of inner strife; a state of untroubled, undisturbed well-being; a tranquil spirit; harmony with another.

Jesus is called the "Prince of Peace" (Isa. 9:6) and the "Lord of Peace" (2 Thess. 3:16). Through Jesus, we can have "peace with God" (Rom. 5:1). The cross removed the barrier of sin that separated us from Him and from one another. The cross "destroyed the barrier" (Eph. 2:14), and "put to death their hostility" that keeps us apart (v. 17).

Jesus gave us the gift of His peace (see John 14:28). He leads us in peace (see Isa. 54:10-12), establishes us in peace (see Isa. 26:12), and keeps us in perfect peace (see Isa. 26:3) as we focus on Him. His peace gives us peace. For that reason, we are encouraged to "seek peace and pursue it" (1 Pet. 3:11), "promote peace" (Prov. 12:20), and to be peacemakers in our relationships (see Eph. 4:3; Heb. 12:14).

Peace contributes to the quality and enjoyment of our lives. Do you remember your Breath Freshener from week 1? First Peter 3:10-11 says that whoever would love life and see good days must seek God's peace and pursue it. But how do we pursue peace? In the same passage as that memory verse, Peter provides the answer. Here is a summary of 1 Peter 3:8-18.

Place a check beside peaceful traits you want to cultivate.

- ❑ Live in harmony, be sympathetic, love as brothers, be compassionate and humble.
- ❑ Don't repay evil with evil or insult with insult, but with blessing.
- ❑ Ask Jesus to fill you with peace and take away your defensive or combative spirit.
- ❑ Know that, in most cases, people will respond well to your peaceable spirit.
- ❑ Be prepared and willing to suffer for doing good. Don't be afraid of how people might treat you. Don't fear being taken advantage of or not having your needs met.
- ❑ Set apart Christ as Lord, recognizing Him as sovereign.
- ❑ Be prepared to tell people that Jesus is the source of your peace.
- ❑ Speak with gentleness and respect.
- ❑ Know that it is better to be verbally abused for being a peacemaker than to do battle and sin with your mouth.
- ❑ Remember that Christ's sacrifice opened the way of peace for you.

> *"Open the gates that the righteous nation [people] may enter, the nation [people] that keeps faith. You will keep in perfect peace him whose mind is steadfast, because he trusts in you."*
> Isaiah 26:2-3

This week's Tongue Tonics will teach you how to use three tools of the trade–the question, statement, and forecast–as tools (the ploughshare) instead of weapons (the sword). When we use these tools in the right way, we assume the role of farmer, not warrior.

Three Tools of the Trade

Imagine trying to paint a wall with a hammer or pounding a nail with a can of paint. Effective communicators know which tool to use and when and how to use it.

1. **THE QUESTION**: a tool for gathering information.
   It is used to help people openly share their thoughts, feelings, and opinions.
2. **THE STATEMENT:** a tool for transmitting information.
   It helps us to openly and clearly express our own feelings, beliefs, opinions, and interpretations.
3. **THE FORECAST**: a tool for outlining future intent. It defines boundaries and consequences: "If you … then I'll."

Unfortunately, we misuse these tools. We ask questions to communicate opinions, make statements to judge and attack, and forecast our intentions to manipulate. Used improperly, these tools become weapons that wreak relationships.

Knowing how we ought to use these tools is not enough. If our hearts are not right, no amount of scripting will enable us to respond in the right way. **Humility** is the central key that enables us to ask pure questions, make honest statements, and forecast in a way that is protective and fair.

Day Two

The High Gate of Control

... is opened with the key of relinquishment.

"'God oppose the proud but gives grace to the humble.' Humble yourselves before the Lord, and he will lift you up."
James 4:6,10

My three teenagers are teaching me a lot about communication. Perhaps it would be more accurate to say that I am learning a lot about my weaknesses. Recently my oldest son, Clark, challenged me by saying: "Mom, can I answer freely, or are you going to keep badgering me until I give you the answer you want to hear? I don't think you're listening to me. I think you're just trying to force me to agree with you. In fact, I find it very hard to talk to you because it seems that all you are concerned about is being proved right!"

Ouch! The truth stung like peroxide on a fresh wound. The Holy Spirit pulled the infected flesh apart so it could seep in. I was made aware of the deep, arrogant fissure in my heart–and I was shamed and grieved. Clark was right. I wasn't listening to him. I was trying to control him, to force him to think and behave a certain way–my way. I was unwilling to consider the situation from his point of view. In my self-righteousness, I had put up a high gate of control that had created a barrier between us.

Erecting the Gate

A gate of control is erected when we seek to manipulate, trap, or coerce others into agreeing with our perspective. The key of relinquishment demolishes the high gate of control. *To relinquish* means "to give up possession of." We humbly recognize that all knowledge, strength and greatness, as well as the right to rule, belong to God and not to us. We cannot lay claim to any of these things.

Let me say at the outset that relinquishment does not mean that we regard all opinions as equally valid–the mind-set that is culturally vogue at this point in history. All opinions aren't equally valid. The Bible clearly teaches that truth and falsehood exist. Through grace, I have bound myself to follow, teach, defend, and proclaim God's truth. I would never want to compromise or relinquish it. In my better moments, I would even be willing to die for it.

What I must relinquish is the prideful attitude that says: "I know truth fully. Truth belongs to me. I am smarter, stronger, and better than you, so do what I say!" No. In relinquishment I place truth on the table with trembling hands, acutely aware that the grain I offer I receive from the Giver's stores and that my small pockets can hold but a miniscule portion of His bounty.

In 1 Corinthians 4:10, Paul pours peroxide on the attitude of some of the Corinthian believers. He points out three ways in which they regard themselves as superior. Fill in the blanks:

1. The apostles were foolish but they were _____.
   [Knowledge]
2. The apostles were weak but they were _____.
   [Strength]
3. They were worthy of greater _____ than the apostles. [Greatness]

   The Corinthians were locked in a battle of opinions about leaders. Some followed Paul, while others gave their allegiance to Apollos or Cephas (see 1 Cor. 1:12; 3:4). Because of these "divisions" (1 Cor. 1:10), they fought, debated, and quarreled over whose position was better.
   According to 1 Corinthians 4:5-8, the Corinthians were
   • casting judgment on the faithfulness and motives of others;
   • going beyond what was written in Scripture;
   • comparing—taking pride in one man's position over another;
   • boasting. In arrogance they regarded themselves as "rich." They thought they were smarter (knowledge), more right (strength) and nobler (greatness) than those with whom they disagreed;
   • claiming the right to rule. They sought to control, manipulate, and impose their opinion on others.

Of all marvelous things, perhaps there is nothing that angels behold with such supreme astonishment as a proud man.
—Charles Caleb Colton

   The problem the Corinthians encountered is not unlike the problems we encounter in our relationships today. The Corinthians had engaged in a power struggle over whose opinion would prevail. They had erected high, proud gates of control. Whenever we enter a discussion with the goal of having others recognize our superior knowledge, strength or greatness—and push to have our opinion prevail—we put up the same kind of barrier.

Demolishing the Gate

How do we tear down the high gate of control? Two actions are required: relinquishing our claim to superiority and relinquishing our right to rule others by coercion, manipulation, or force.

Jeremiah 9:23-24 shows how we can relinquish our claim to superiority. Draw lines to match the items in the two columns:

Wise Person   should not boast in his or her riches
Strong Person   should boast in the Lord
Rich Person   should not boast in his or her strength
Anyone who boasts   should not boast in his or her wisdom

The Hebrew word translated *boast* means "to glory in." We display it, hold it up, and show it off to others so that they, too, will recognize its splendor and superiority. In short, we brag on it. According to the verses we just read, we should not exalt our own intellect, abilities, or position but should "brag on" the Lord.

Jeremiah bragged about the Lord's kindness, justice, and righteousness. In 1 Chronicles 29:11-12, David bragged about some of God's other attributes. Write these below.

_____

_____

Paul reminded the Corinthians that "the foolishness of God is wiser than man's wisdom, and the weakness of God is stronger than man's strength" (1 Cor. 1:25). Compared to God, none of us—even the "greatest" by human standards—amounts to anything. God alone is "Most High over all the earth" (Ps. 83:18). He alone is "King" (Ps. 29:10; 95:3).

When we set ourselves up as "king" and "most high," we assault truth and dishonor God by pretending to fill shoes that only He can fill. But when we relinquish our claim to superiority and fall to our faces in humility, we affirm truth. We honor God for who He is.

Humble people relinquish the right to control. They are acutely aware of their own fallibility when it comes to judging correctly (see Rom. 2:1-4). Thus they offer judgments cautiously, with a humble rather than a demanding spirit. They relinquish the right to arrogantly coerce or force others to agree with their opinions.

Read Romans 14:10-13. Why should I relinquish the right to control someone by forcing her to agree with me?
❑ Otherwise, she would resent me.
❑ It would result in a power struggle.
❑ I don't want things to get ugly.
❑ Ultimately, she answers to God and not to me.

If you put up a high gate of control by bragging on your own wisdom, strength, riches or position, and try to coerce or manipulate others to do things your way, God will oppose you and, at some point, "bring you down." If, on the other hand, you open your gate, relinquish your pride, and bow low before God, He will lift you up and clothe you in wisdom, strength, riches, and honor (see Prov. 3:24; Luke 14:11). The choice is yours: honor yourself, or be honored by Him. Bar your gate in pride, or in humility throw it wide open.

Do you use questions to control and manipulate others rather than to genuinely request information or seek clarification? Today's Tongue Tonic will help you take the control out of your questions.

The Question: A Quest for Information

A non-defensive question invites others to share thoughts, feelings, and beliefs without fearing we will use the information against them. A non-defensive question is:

INNOCENT: not tainted with underlying opinions or agendas; eager to learn and understand; has no goal beyond wanting to clarify the other person's perspective.

NEUTRAL: calm and relaxed; making the tone of one's voice stay the same or go down at the end of the question—instead of going up; gives the hearer permission to respond honestly, without feeling asked for a specific response.

FOCUSED: puts the other person in the spotlight and focuses on seeing things from her point of view; focuses on: "What is this person thinking and feeling and why?"

OPEN: a genuine invitation for the other person to speak honestly about what she thinks and feels; indicates that the asker is open to hearing even negative feedback.

Ask yourself whether your questions are typically non-defensive:
  I: Are they innocent and curious, free of opinions and agendas?
  N: Is my voice neutral? Am I feeling calm and relaxed?
  F: Am I focused on the speaker and not on myself?
  O: Am I open to hearing the answer? Have I given up control?

Counterfeit Questions

A question is counterfeit whenever it does anything other than invite people to share openly. Here are common types of counterfeits:

1. State an Opinion: A question that subtly presents an underlying opinion is a counterfeit question. For example, the underlying message of the question, "What did you do that for?" is, "I don't think you should have."

2. Hide an Agenda: Counterfeit questions carry hidden agendas. The question, "Don't you have homework tonight?" may carry the agenda, "I want you to turn off the TV." "Isn't that music too loud?" may indicate, "I want you to turn it down."

3. Require the *correct* answer: A question is counterfeit when it is phrased in such a way that it leads to the response the asker wants to hear. What do you think the asker wants to hear when she inquires, "Do you think I look good in this dress?"

4. Present No-Win Choices: Questions can be phrased in such a way that they offer a choice of no-win responses. Amy asked Jack, "Are you planning on being late again or are you going to think about someone other than yourself?" Jack is in a no-win situation. Either answer incriminates him.

5. Set a Trap: Questions can be used as clever weapons to entrap others. Consider the question, "Do you want to know a better way to do that?" If we say no, we indicate that we are unwilling to learn. If we say yes, we acknowledge that the other person's way is better before we even know what it is. Most of us are unable to think fast enough to respond without entangling ourselves.

Avoid counterfeit questions. Instead, use questions in the proper way to open up channels of communication.

Day Three
The High Gate of Assumption
... is opened with the key of understanding.

"If you call out for insight and cry aloud for understanding, and if you look for it as for silver and search for it as for hidden treasure, then you will understand the fear of the Lord and find the knowledge of God."
Proverbs 2:3-5

Flight 985 was en route from Miami to Colombia with 164 people on board—most of them going home for Christmas—when it slammed into a mountain 40 miles south of Cali. Investigators suspect the crash was caused by language problems between the American crew and the Colombian air traffic controllers.

As we learned in this week's Talk Show, language barriers originated at the Tower of Babel. God confused people's language so they would "not understand each other" (Gen. 11:7). This lack of understanding is not limited to different languages. Those who speak the same language frequently have difficulty understanding one another.

Like me, I suspect you encounter this problem on an ongoing basis. We make assumptions, jump to conclusions, fail to listen, interpret words differently, and bring all sorts of personal baggage into the communication process. In pride, we put up high gates of assumption, thinking that we understand perfectly when we really don't. In today's lesson, we will see that the high gate of assumption is brought down with the key of understanding.

Characteristics of Assumption
Read Isaiah 6:9-10. How did Isaiah describe their problem?
❏ They were hearing impaired.
❏ They needed high-powered glasses.
❏ They could hear well, but couldn't understand.
❏ They had good vision, but couldn't perceive.

What was wrong with their senses (see v. 10)? Fill in the blanks:
Their hearts were   Their ears were   Their eyes were

_____   _____   _____

The people lacked understanding. Their hearts were calloused, their ears were dull, and their eyes were closed. In Scripture, *to understand* means "to bring together, as foes in battle; to collect together, apprehend, grasp, comprehend; to lay to heart."

God is the source of all understanding (see Isa. 40:28). "His understanding has no limit" (Ps. 147:5). "All the treasures" of understanding are hidden in Him (Col. 2:3). Compared to Him, humans know nothing at all. Therefore, true understanding is based on one thing and one thing only: knowledge of God.

We understand God when we apprehend and grasp His plan of salvation and are brought into a relationship with Him (justification). We grow in understanding as we get to know Him better and become more like Him (sanctification).

You're not listening ... well, your heart is not.
—Merlin in Excalibur

God is able to discern the thoughts and motivations of people's hearts. As we become more like Him, we become more apt to discern and understand. Our ability to understand people is therefore inseparably related to our relationship to God.

Those who are not in relationship with God are said to have a "darkened" understanding. The Bible commonly refers to them as "fools."

"Knowledge of the Holy One is understanding."
Proverbs 9:10

How does a fool's lack of understanding show up in communication? Underline the negative effects in these verses:

"He is conceited and understands nothing. He has an unhealthy interest in controversies and quarrels about words that result in envy, strife, malicious talk, evil suspicions and constant friction between men of corrupt mind, who have been robbed of the truth" (1 Tim. 6:4-5).

"The woman Folly is loud; she is undisciplined and without knowledge" (Prov. 9:13).

"A fool finds no pleasure in understanding but delights in airing his own opinions" (Prov. 18:2).

"They are darkened in their understanding and separated from the life of God because of the ignorance that is in them due to the hardening of their hearts."
Ephesians 4:18

Those without knowledge
- are conceited. They assume they know it all. They take delight in airing their own opinions and do not seek understanding;
- are "loud, undisciplined, and without knowledge";
- engage in "controversies, quarrels about words, envy, strife, malicious talk, evil suspicions and constant friction."

This attitude stands in marked contrast to the behavior of a person with understanding.

Characteristics of Understanding

What characterizes a person of understanding? Write the characteristic found in each verse:

1. Proverbs 9:9 _____

2. Proverbs 11:12 _____

3. Proverbs 14:29 _____

4. Proverbs 15:14 _____

Understanding demolishes the high gate of assumption. Those with understanding are
- humble, pleasant, and approachable;
- aware they don't know it all; eager to be corrected;
- good listeners; ask questions to help them discern correctly;
- deliberate. They weigh their words before responding.

Read below the characteristics of foolishness and understanding. Then put an "X" on the scale to indicate how you approach conversations. (Our most challenging relationships have a way of flushing out what's really in our hearts.)

The Way of Foolishness	The Way of Understanding
I am full of pride.	I am full of humility.
I engage in quarrels and controversy.	I hold my tongue.
I have evil suspicions.	I do not make assumptions.
I experience friction.	I am pleasant and approachable.
I am loud and undisciplined.	I am patient and listen diligently.
I speak without knowledge.	I seek and discern knowledge.
I delight in my own opinion.	I delight in understanding you.
I assume I understand you.	I need you to instruct me.
I am above correction.	I am willing to be corrected.

Every man is superior to me in some way and from him I can learn.
—Ralph Waldo Emerson

If dealing with people in an understanding way is difficult for you, remember that through Christ we have an abundance of understanding at our disposal. He provides the feast. Our part is simply to come to Him with an appetite.

Do you hunger for understanding? Do you "cry aloud" for it and "look for it as for silver and search for it as for hidden treasure" (Prov. 2:3-4)? Close today's lesson by asking God to increase your appetite. As your desire and ability to understand increases, your high gates of assumption will be demolished, and you will begin to notice positive changes in your speech.

Making a Statement

The statement is used to openly and clearly express our own feelings, opinions, and interpretations. You can use a "PhD" to evaluate your statements.

Personal: Statements express our personal point of view. Problems occur when we state our opinions as all-knowing, objective facts. "You are so stubborn!" "They shouldn't do that!" "It won't work." A good statement presents personal opinion as personal opinion and not as universal truth. It uses qualifiers such as, "In my opinion," or "As I see it ... " A good statement does not force others to agree. It is not dominating, and it is non-defensive.

Honest: Good statements honestly (but tactfully) express what we are thinking and feeling. They are inherently open and self-revealing. They open my heart and allow others to see the real me. People are not left wondering if what they are seeing is genuine.

Direct: Good statements are free from hidden motives and meanings. We do not hint or "beat around the bush." Instead, we state our needs, desires, and goals directly.

The appropriate level of self-disclosure does differ. It is neither wise nor appropriate to indiscriminately reveal the thoughts of our hearts. Some thoughts are best left unspoken. Some relationships do not warrant high levels of disclosure. Nevertheless, though the level of self-disclosure varies, it is possible to be **personal, honest,** and **direct** with the information we do choose to communicate.

The Threefold RAP Statement

A helpful format for making clear, open statements is the "RAP."

Report: Convey your observations about the other person's verbal, vocal, and visual behavior. "I see ..." "You said ... "

Analyze: We provide an analysis of what the message means to us, including what we perceive to be the underlying cause or motive. "Then I think ..." "I assume ..." "I interpret that to mean ... "

Personalize: We express our personal experience—our own reactions, thoughts, and feelings. "I feel ..." "I am ... "

The **RAP** format is particularly helpful when giving someone feedback on what you perceive to be a mixed message. Using a **RAP** to express feelings, thoughts, and needs does not necessarily create a solution, but it does provide clarity—which is the basis for moving toward a solution.

Day Four

The High Gate of Haste

... is opened with the key of patience.

"Be completely humble and gentle; be patient, bearing with one another in love."
Ephesians 4:2

Last year I hurriedly deleted some computer files to free up some extra hard-drive space. Instead of carefully verifying the content and purpose of each file, I quickly went through the DOS list and discarded anything that appeared obsolete or unnecessary.

Those of you who are familiar with computers are already cringing. You know what happened. In haste, I deleted a file that was essential to my operating system and crashed my computer. One moment of haste resulted in two weeks of technical support and trouble-shooting to get my computer working again, and months (in some cases, years) of important files being lost forever. (You guessed it. I hadn't backed up my data–I was in too much of a hurry!)

The ancient philosopher Herodotus once said, "Haste in every business brings failures." All of us have experienced situations where we have not given the necessary time and care to our task and have afterwards regretted the negative consequences of our neglect.

Patience strengthens the spirit, sweetens the temper, stifles anger, subdues pride, and bridles the tongue.
—Author Unknown

What causes haste? The obvious answer is a lack of time. But I believe there is more to haste than that. I was hasty with my computer because I overestimated my ability to discern and make the right decisions about those files. I thought I had the capacity to do it quickly. It was my pride that allowed me to act in careless haste.

Prideful Haste

Pride causes our words to be hasty. We react quickly and carelessly because we are overconfident in our own ability to listen, interpret, and correctly respond to the other person. Haste creates a barrier to true understanding. The writer of Proverbs said, "Do you see a man who speaks in haste? There is more hope for a fool than for him" (29:20).

Read James 1:19. List the three instructions James gave his readers about what they should be "quick" and "slow" to do.

1. _____

2. _____

3. _____

In this verse, James described the three types of behaviors that characterize haste:
1. failure to restrain assumptions (listen)
2. failure to restrain words (speak)
3. failure to restrain emotional responses (anger)

1. Jumping to conclusions is the first sign of haste. Hasty people assume they understand. They are not "quick to listen." They do not inquire, ask for clarification, or check their perceptions. Not only do they fail to listen to other people, they also fail to listen to God. They respond before they take the time to ask Him for wisdom and understanding on how to best handle the situation.

"What you have seen with your eyes do not bring hastily to court, for what will you do in the end if your neighbor puts you to shame?" Proverbs 25:7-8

When we are hasty, we are very susceptible to errors in judgment. We can easily "miss the way." Proverbs 19:2 says, "It is not good to have zeal without knowledge, nor to be hasty and miss the way."

The person referred to in Proverbs 25:8 drew the wrong conclusions from what he had observed ("seen with your eyes"). Instead of checking his perceptions, he accused his neighbor of wrongdoing ("bring hastily to court"). In the end, the neighbor was exonerated, and the accuser put to shame for his presumptuousness.

Have you ever felt shamed about jumping to the wrong conclusions? Last week, my girlfriend was angry with her husband for his apparent insensitivity in coming home late. Imagine her shame, when after reviling and maligning him, he produced the reason for his delay: a huge bouquet of flowers. He was tardy because he had stopped at the florist shop on the way home to surprise her. She had jumped to the wrong conclusion.

2. Haste is also characterized by a failure to restrain words.

Read Proverbs 15:28. What do the wise do before speaking? (Circle the correct picture.)

"The heart of the righteous weighs its answers, but the mouth of the wicked gushes evil." Proverbs 15:28

The wise weigh their words before they speak. They "give thought to their ways" (Prov. 14:8). They speak "with restraint" (Prov. 17:27) because they know that there is a time to speak and a time to remain silent (see Prov. 12:23). They do not talk excessively for they know that "when words are many, sin is not absent" (Prov. 10:19).

3. Haste is characterized by a failure to restrain anger (see Prov. 14:16). When a perceived right is violated, or a felt need unmet, many of us respond in anger. Anger is not sin. Anger is an emotion just as joy, hurt, disappointment, hope, and frustration are emotions. But anger often points to a sinful attitude or belief. It is such a powerful emotion that it can easily lead to sins such as bitterness, brawling, malice, slander, and destructive speech (see Eph. 4:26-31). James instructs us to be "slow to become angry, for man's anger does not bring about the righteous life that God desires" (Jas 1:19-20).

How does the way foolish people conduct themselves in conversation differ from the way wise people conduct themselves? Fill in the following chart:

Scripture Passage	The Foolish Person	The Wise Person
Proverbs 12:16		
Proverbs 12:23		
Proverbs 20:3		
Proverbs 29:11		

Patience Overcomes Haste

Nothing is so full of victory as patience.
—Chinese Proverb

A wise person opens the high gate of haste with the key of patience. Patience can overcome the unrestrained assumptions, words, and anger of haste.

Read today's Word from the Word to learn more about the virtue of patience.

[patience] The Ability to Bear Up Under

The word *patient* is formed by two Greek words: *hupo*, "under," and *meno*, to abide. To be patient is to "bear up /abide under." Biblical patience is a God-given restraint that allows an individual to calmly abide pain or trial without complaining or retaliating. Patience is not passive. It involves waiting with self-disciplined calmness, diligence, and perseverance. The word is closely related to two other words: *forbearance* (to hold up or hold back) and *longsuffering* (long of temper; to show merciful self-restraint).

God is the God of Patience (see Rom. 15:5). Jesus displays God's "unlimited patience" (1 Tim. 1:16). Though sinful humanity is fully deserving of His anger, He is slow to punish us because "He is patient with you, not wanting anyone to perish, but everyone to come to repentance" (2 Pet. 3:9).

Paul urged us to "be patient with everyone" (1 Thess. 5:14). God is the One who gives us power and strengthens us to be patient (see Col. 1:11). Patience matures us and gives us hope (see Rom. 5:3-5). Knowing this, we can be joyful and calm when we face difficult people or circumstances (see Jas. 1:2-4). If we are patient, our suffering and our hope will be rewarded.

Having patience with people is particularly difficult when

we are being provoked by their foolish speech or accusations. Somebody accuses us, and immediately we respond in irritation or anger. The writer of Proverbs said being provoked by a fool is worse than having a load of stone or sand carelessly dumped on us (see Prov. 27:3). Our natural response is to get angry and retaliate against the one doing the dumping. If we are wise, we will respond with patience and overlook the assault: "A man's wisdom gives him patience; it is to his glory to overlook an offense" (Prov. 19:11).

Proverbs 16:32 says, "Better a patient man than a warrior, a man who controls his temper than one who takes a city." When we respond in haste to defend our territory, we become a warrior. In self-defense, we retaliate –fortify our gate–and dare our opponents to strike again. One provocation leads to another, and before we know it, we are engaged in a full-scale war. No wonder the Bible says, "Better a patient man than a warrior."

I pray, as Paul did, that you may be strengthened "with all power according to his glorious might so that you may have great endurance and patience, and joyfully giving thanks to the Father, who has qualified you to share in the inheritance" (Col. 1:11-12). "Father, full of grace and truth" (John 1:14). You see, God's Word is His communication to you. Are you listening to His special message?

Forecast: Your Statement of Intent

The forecast communicates our future intent. It defines boundaries and consequences for behavior. It forecasts, "If this happens … then I will react like that." A forecast defines very precisely how we will respond to the choices others make.

When my children were struggling with early morning procrastination last year, I forecast: "I will be leaving at exactly 8:30 a.m. tomorrow morning. I will call you once at 8:25 to remind you. If you are not dressed, ready to go, and at the door by 8:30, I will leave without you, and you will have to get to school on your own." My children knew the precise consequences of their choices. If they were ready, they would get a ride with me; if they were late, they would not.

The morning after my forecast, two of my children were ready to go to school at 8:30, and one was not. I knew that the tardy one had an important class first thing in the morning, but I also knew that I needed to act as I had forecast. So at the appointed time, I drove off and left him (he rode his bike to school in the snow). Having a precise, predictable consequence freed me from responding in anger. I was able to act calmly with the behavior I had predicted. It protected my son from feeling he had been blindsided. I had forecast my behavior. He knew the consequences of his actions.

Forecasts should be (1) **personal** (how we will respond),
(2) **protective** (others know what to expect of us rather than being blindsided), (3) **precise** (how we respond in descriptive terms), and
(4) **predictable** (follow-through on our forecasts).

Day Five

The High Gate of Entitlement

... is opened with the key of self-sacrifice.

"The sacrifices of God are a broken spirit; a broken and contrite heart, O God, you will not despise."
Psalm 51:17

We live in a culture that focuses on personal rights–civil rights, women's rights, children's rights, gay rights, student rights, labor rights, prisoner's rights–the list goes on and on. The focus on rights is based on the conviction that all people are equal. From this conviction comes the notion that all people are therefore owed an equal entitlement.

While the Bible certainly upholds the equal worth and dignity of people, and while I believe this truth must, by necessity, be upheld by law, the current focus on rights has–for many of us–introduced a dangerous distortion into our thinking. Instead of focusing on what we can give, we are consumed with concern about what we are entitled to receive.

I tremble as I write, for I know how deeply this attitude of entitlement is ingrained in our psyche. To challenge it is akin to questioning whether the sky is blue. The Bible teaches that an attitude of entitlement is the lynchpin of pride. It tells us to put aside our rights, become servants, and willingly sacrifice self.

Christ's Example of Servanthood

Read Philippians 2:5-8. What do these verses teach about Christ's example of servanthood? Check one or more.
❑ Christ is in very nature God.
❑ Christ the Son is equal to God the Father.
❑ Christ willingly let go of the rights to which He was entitled.
❑ Christ "made himself nothing" to be made in human likeness (v. 7).
❑ Christ adopted the attitude and nature of a master.
❑ Christ sacrificed Himself.

Did you check all but the fifth box? Being God, Christ was entitled to everything. Yet instead of demanding His rights, He set them aside, adopted the nature of a servant, and out of obedience to the Father sacrificed Himself for humanity.

Once (or perhaps more than once), while chiding my sons for not keeping their rooms clean, I exclaimed, "Let's get this straight–I am not your servant!" If I am not mistaken, I think I said the same thing to my husband after transporting his extremely stinky sports socks to the laundry bin.

Was my attitude wrong? Does being Christlike require that I become everyone's slave and sacrificially do everything they want?

My sons would truly enjoy it if I did everything for them. I can hear them now: "YES! (High fives all around.) No more dishes! No more cleaning! No more putting away laundry! Mom could even do my homework!" Is that what being a servant means?

In order to understand the biblical concept of servanthood, we must be clear on one critical point. When Christ set aside His rights, He became a servant of God the Father—not a servant of man (see Isa. 42:1; 52:13). He served people, but His servanthood—His self-sacrificial obedience—was to God (see Matt. 12:18-20). Read these last two lines again. They are important.

Also, servanthood is voluntary. Christ chose to submit Himself to the Father. The Father didn't force Him to submit. Paul described his relationship to God as "bondservant," "one who gives himself up to the will of another voluntarily." The term does not carry any over-tones of obligation or bondage. Christ sets us free from bondage to sin so that we are free to "bond" ourselves to Him.

Did Christ become weak, passive, and do whatever people demanded of Him? Many considered His actions offensive. At times, He confronted others harshly. (Remember the whip in the temple?) He became angry. He did not hesitate to call sin "sin" (see Matt. 12:29). He never compromised truth. He never denied who He was. And He never denied that He had rights.

But Christ did do everything His Father wanted. He willingly set aside His rights to obey His Father. He was willing to sacrifice, suf-fer—even die—in obedience to the Father's will. Being a servant of God means setting aside my rights and being willing to do everything that God wants—even if it involves hardship, suffering, and self-sacrifice.

Our Call to Servanthood

God may want you to go the extra mile and endure mistreatment in your interpersonal relationships (see Matt. 5:38-42). He may want you to be patient and "overlook an offense" (Prov. 19:11). Or, He may want you to firmly confront sin and let the person experience the natural consequence of their behavior (see Matt. 18:15-17). He has not given us a cookie-cutter pattern. In every situation we must seek the wisdom and guidance of His Spirit to know what to do.

Not I, but Christ, be honored, loved exalted; Not I, but Christ, be seen, be known, be heard; Not I, but Christ, in every look and action; Not I, but Christ, in every thought and word.
—Author Unknown

In all circumstances and in all relationships we ought to follow Christ's example of servanthood. When I follow Christ's example

- I do not claim what I am entitled to claim; I am willing to "lay down my life" in obedience to God (John 10:17-18).
- I do not conclude what I feel entitled to conclude; I wait to hear the opinion of God (see John 12:47-49).

- I do not say what I feel entitled to say; I only say what God tells me to say (see John 12:49).
- I do not do what I feel entitled to do; I only do what God tells me to do (see John 14:31).
- I do not walk where I am entitled to walk; I only follow where He leads (see Mark 14:36).
- I do not put up a high gate of entitlement; I open my door with self-sacrifice (see Phil. 2:6-7).

Think of a meaningful relationship. What are some rights to which you feel entitled, such as the right to express your opinion or make your own decision? Now consider your responsibility.

According to Philippians 2:3-5, our responsibility is fourfold:
- To avoid trying to "get ahead" ("selfish ambition")
- To refrain from thinking I am better in some way ("vain conceit" vs. "humility")
- To carefully consider the other person's interests and point of view
- To be willing to sacrifice self out of obedience to God

Read 1 Peter 3:14. What can prevent us from giving up our rights and imitating the servanthood of Christ?

_____

"But even if you should suffer for what is right, you are blessed. 'Do not fear what they fear; do not be frightened.'"
1 Peter 3:14

Setting aside our rights makes us vulnerable. Others might hurt us or take advantage of our humble posture. Fear can prevent us from imitating Christ's servanthood. In 1 Peter 2:22 we are told how Jesus managed to remain calm and resolute. When Christ set aside His rights in obedience to the Father, He was not left unprotected. He knew that He could trust the Father to be His defender and protector. He knew that although He would suffer, He would ultimately triumph. Victory was certain. He could trust His Father.

The Philippians 2:3-11 passage begins with Christ bowing very low, but it ends with the Father exalting and lifting Christ to the highest place, forcing all the powers of the universe to bow at His feet. In the end, the power of Christ crushes the power of Satan. Humility triumphs over arrogance. Self-sacrifice triumphs over entitlement.

"When they hurled their insults at him, he did not retaliate; when he suffered, he made no threats. Instead, he entrusted himself to him who judges justly."
1 Peter 2:23

Every lesson this week has addressed the two opposing attitudes of pride and humility. Most of the problems we encounter in communication are problems of pride. Pride sets up high gates of battle, control, assumption, haste, and entitlement, creating seemingly insurmountable barriers in relationships.

Jesus demonstrated that the way to victory is the way of the cross. The barriers in our relationships are not insurmountable. Through humility, we can begin to demolish them. Humility lowers the drawbridge, raises the bars, and throws open the doors of our castles to unleash the power of the open gate.

Make a Fair Forecast

Normally, forecasts involve recurring patterns in relationships. We must carefully consider any forecasts we make because they may have broad impact on the way a relationship functions. We must ensure that we are willing to live with the consequences if the other person chooses not to respond in the way we would prefer. Problems occur when we make impulsive, manipulative threats or promises that we are unwilling and/or unable to carry out.

Before making a forecast, inventory the specifics that are causing the problem. Identify what the other person does, how you react, and the core issues and motivators at work in the situation. Come up with a list of how you could respond (feel, believe, or act), and then choose the consequence most appropriate for the situation. For example, Angie decides that she doesn't like for her roommate, Margaret, to constantly leave dirty dishes in the sink. Angie forecasts, "If you leave dishes unwashed in the sink, then before I go to bed, I will put them in a bucket under the sink for you to wash the next day" (first forecast). "If I find that I do not have clean dishes and pots when I need them, then I will designate certain dishes and pots to you and not allow you to use mine" (second forecast). With these forecasts, Angie establishes boundaries with which she is comfortable and allows Margaret the freedom to choose how to respond.

Before we forecast a consequence, we must ensure that we are willing to follow through. Angie must be willing to let the dirty dishes sit in the bucket under the sink and not break down and wash them. If we decide we can't live with the possible ramifications, we must choose a different consequence. Making a forecast such as, "If you hang up, I'll never talk to you again!" is unreasonable and unrealistic. The consequence needs to be trimmed to a much smaller size.

Forecasts are intended to clearly state our intentions so the other person can make an informed choice regarding their behavior. Therefore, put all the consequences into the forecast and do not add any after the fact. (Though you may choose to make a new forecast after carrying through on the old one.) For example, Angie forecast that she would store Margaret's dirty dishes in a bucket under the sink. If she also reacts by feeling angry, resentful, and by withdrawing from the relationship, she is adding unstated consequences to the deal.

When you have decided on a consequence, don't forget to self-check your verbal, vocal, and visual behavior to ensure that you communicate your forecast in a non-combative, non-defensive manner. When following through on a forecast, do so in a timely manner with firmness and consistency. Avoid negotiating, arguing, or changing the consequence.

Tools Instead of Weapons

Use the three tools of the trade–the question, statement, and forecast–as plowshares instead of swords. We cultivate rather than attack and defend. We are focused on promoting growth and not on winning a battle. When used as tools our words are filled with truth, openness, and wisdom instead of deceit, hidden meaning, and folly.

The Power of Construction

Hearts connect when words build tracks of love.

Do your words cross barriers or create them? Do they put up obstacles or *lay tracks* to help you connect with others? Loving words move people closer together. This week you can begin to experience greater harmony in your relationships by harnessing the power of construction to build tracks of love.

Sir John A. MacDonald had a dream to build a transcontinental railway connecting the provinces of Canada. Our words can lay tracks to connect us to one another with strong bonds of friendship and unity. In this week's Talk Show, we'll take a look at how to achieve that dream.

Day 1: Lay Tracks of Nourishment
  ... *with ties of support, affirmation, and encouragement.*
Day 2: Lay Tracks of Faithfulness
  ... *with ties of loyalty, commitment, and devotion.*
Day 3: Lay Tracks of Honesty
  ... *with ties of openheartedness, authenticity, and truth.*
Day 4: Lay Tracks of Tenderheartedness
  ... *with ties of kindness, compassion, and forgiveness.*
Day 5: Lay Tracks of Discretion
  ... *with ties of discernment, prudence, and good judgment.*

This Week's Tongue Tonics:
  • It's a Dogfight
  • Conflict Chain
  • It's Your Problem
  • Resolve Conflict
  • Bypass the Bait
  • Resist Manipulation

"Do not let any unwholesome talk come out of your mouths, but only what is helpful for building others up according to their needs, that it may benefit those who listen" (Eph. 4:29).

Cut out the Scripture card on page 147 as a reminder.

The Power of Construction: Laying tracks to connect
Ephesians 4:20–5:4

This Talk Show guide will help you follow the video for Session Five.

1. Embrace the vision.

In the Book of Ephesians, Paul's vision for our speech is a vision for:

a. something _____ (see 4:22-24).

b. _____ (see 4:25)–all members of one body working in cooperation.

c. spiritual _____ (see 4:27,30)–defeat for evil and triumph for God.

2. Overcome barriers.

a. Selfish _____ (4:22) replaced by working in cooperation.

b. _____ (4:25) replaced by truthful speech.

c. _____ (see 4:31; 5:4) replaced even when the going is slow.

d. _____ to pay the price (see 5:1-2) replaced by sacrificial imitation of God.

3. Lay track (see 4:29).

a. Wholesome words are like good _____.

b. Helpful words are focused on the needs of _____

c. Beneficial words lay track for God's _____ in the lives of others.

*With the power of construction, your words
can build into a kingdom that will last forever.*

Day One

Lay Tracks of Nourishment

... with ties of support, affirmation, and encouragement.

"My purpose is that they may be encouraged in heart and united in love."
Colossians 2:2

His mother was not home, but the young boy wanted to draw, so he got out the bottles of ink and enlisted his sister as a model. The young artist made an inky mess of his hands, clothes, table, and floor. Just as he was finishing his work, his mother returned. For a moment, she stood in the door and silently took in the scene. Then, instead of scolding him, she picked up the portrait and declared, "What a beautiful picture of your sister!" and kissed him. Later in life, the great artist Benjamin West recounted, "With that kiss, I became a painter."[1]

It would have been so easy for that mother to focus on the mess or his impatience at not waiting for her assistance. Instead, she affirmed him. With her encouragement, he gained the desire, confidence, and determination to become a great painter. In today's lesson we will see how our words can nourish others and give them the desire, confidence, and determination to do great things.

Reasons to Be An Encourager

Use the following verse to complete the crossword puzzle:

"The tongue of the righteous is choice silver, but the heart of the wicked is of little value. The lips of the righteous nourish many, but fools die for lack of judgment" (Prov. 10:20-21).

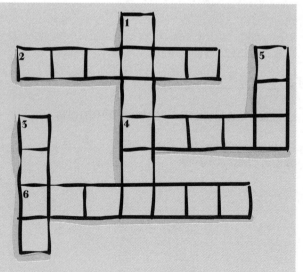

Down
1. The righteous tongue is this type of precious metal.
3. How many people benefit from one righteous tongue?
5. What do fools do?

Across
2. Of what quality is the silver?
4. The heart of the wicked has little of this.
6. What do the lips of the righteous do?

Righteous lips lay tracks of nourishment. *To nourish* means, "to feed and cause to grow; to cherish, promote, encourage and support." Encouragement tells the other person: "I value you. I want you to succeed. I am cheering for you. Keep going! You can do it!"

In the Bible, there are many examples of people who encouraged others. Moses encouraged Joshua (see Deut. 3:28), Titus encouraged Paul (see 2 Cor. 7:4), Tychicus encouraged the believers at Ephesus (see Eph. 6:21-22), Judas and Silas encouraged the church in Jerusalem (see Acts 15:32), and Timothy encouraged the Thessalonians (see 1 Thess. 3:2). A man named Joseph was such an encourager that the apostles nicknamed him *Barnabas* which means "Son of Encouragement" (Acts 4:36).

Correction does much, but encouragement does more.
—Johann Wolfgang Von Goethe

In 1 Thessalonians 5:11, what are we told to do?

_____

According to Hebrews 3:13, how often should we encourage one another?

❑ every minute
❑ every week

❑ every day
❑ every once in a while

Paul wanted believers to encourage one another daily "and all the more" as time went by (Heb. 10:25). He viewed encouragement as so important that he sent messengers great distances for the express purpose of encouraging the believers. Why is encouragement so important? What does encouragement do for people? According to the Bible:

- It "build[s] up" (1 Thess. 5:11).
- It makes people feel loved, appreciated, and supported (see 2 Cor. 7:13, 1 Thess. 3:2; Philem. 7).
- It strengthens people to do good deeds and works (see 2 Thess. 2:16-17).
- It helps people "remain true to the Lord" (Acts 11:23).
- It gives courage (see 2 Chron. 32:6-7; Phil. 1:14).
- It counters feelings of isolation and contributes to "a spirit of unity" (Rom. 15:5; see also 1 Thess. 3:6-10).
- It gives joy and strength in the face of difficulty (see 2 Cor. 7:4,7).
- It helps them to remain true to their calling (see Deut. 1:38).
- It helps them retain perspective and to hope and trust in God (see 2 Chron. 32:6-7).

One word of encouragement can lift our burdens and turn our gloom into sunshine and our weakness into strength. Still so often, we fail to encourage one another. Have you ever felt like giving up because of a lack of encouragement? I have. The moment I most needed encouragement all I received was criticism. Instead of rejoicing in the picture I was trying so hard to paint, others merely pointed to the ink that I spilled. Then I felt like throwing away the canvas.

"Encourage one another and build each other up, just as in fact you are doing."
1 Thessalonians 5:11

"Encourage one another daily, as long as it is called Today, so that none of you may be hardened by sin's deceitfulness."
Hebrews 3:13

Obstacles to Encouragement

Why do we criticize rather than encourage others? The **biggest obstacle** to encouragement is envy. We compare ourselves to others and begrudge what God has given them. We are filled with discontent, resentment, malice, and insecurity. (Feeling threatened is most often a problem of envy.) We don't love and accept others as being valuable parts of the body. We don't want them to be recognized or to succeed. Instead, we wish them to fail.

Envy caused the religious leaders to begrudge the success of Jesus. Envy led them to criticize Him, to plot His downfall, and to rejoice in His demise (see Matt. 27:18; Mark 15:10). They came up with religious-sounding reasons, but envy prevented them from accepting, loving, and encouraging Him. How often have we contributed to the downfall and demise of our Christian brothers and sisters with our silence, our lack of support, or our active criticism? I shudder to think of it.

A **second obstacle** is failure to appreciate its importance. The Bible reaffirms the importance of encouragement. A **third obstacle** is lack of knowledge. We simply do not know what we can do to encourage others. Scripture gives us a few ideas.

As you read, check the items you feel comfortable doing.
❑ Be interested and concerned about what is happening in other people's lives. Be eager to discover their interests (see Phil. 2:1-4).
❑ Ask God to give you some spiritual gift with which to strengthen them (see Rom. 1:11).
❑ Meet together and interact with them (see Heb. 10:25).
❑ Ask questions about how and what they are doing (see 2 Cor. 7:7; 1 Thess. 3:5).
❑ Tell them that you love and support them (see 2 Cor. 7:4, Philem. 7).
❑ Express appreciation and tell them how they bless you (see 2 Cor. 8:3-4; Phil 4:10).
❑ Tell them you want them to succeed (see Col. 1:28–2:2).
❑ Pass along encouraging messages from others (see 1 Thess. 3:7).
❑ Tell them you are praying for them and do not fail to do so (see 1 Thess. 3:2-3).
❑ Encourage them to pursue their dreams. Be excited about new ideas. Look for practical ways to help (see Acts 18:27).
❑ Take initiative to see and meet their needs, especially their financial needs (see Acts 4:32-35).

Did you notice that encouragement is mostly expressed through words? Encouragement doesn't take much effort or time. That's why we are able to do it daily.

Think of three people you would like to encourage over the next week. Write their names below. (Consider encouraging someone you have previously failed to encourage.)

1. _____ 2. _____ 3. _____

Choose one of the people and resolve to encourage him or her consistently over the next six months: weekly–or even daily. See what happens. You'll be surprised how much your relationship grows. Now I want to encourage you with a thought based on 2 Chronicles 32:7-8:

> "Be strong and courageous. Do not be afraid or discouraged" because of the immensity of the task before you, "for there is a greater power" with you than against you. With you is the power of the Lord your God to help you gain victory. He will help you overcome barriers and build tracks to connect with the ones you love. He will transform your speech and bring you more and more *conversation peace.*

It's a Dogfight

Unfortunately, conflicts are often like dogfights. Instead of resolving the conflict honestly and openly, parties engage in aggressive and defensive behavior. Fighting behavior falls under three dog-like categories: rollover, hide, and bite.

ROLLOVER RETRIEVER: When faced with conflict, the Rollover Retriever chooses a passive way of protecting herself. She rolls over and gives in to the other person's opinions and desires, rationalizing or resenting the fact that she has rolled over. If she rationalizes, she blames herself for the problem and/or excuses the other person's behavior. If she resents complying, she is motivated to strike back. So she retaliates in a subversive manner, attacking the underbelly by resisting, procrastinating, maligning, and/or undermining her opponent–a passive-aggressive method of dealing with conflict.

HIDING HOUND: When he feels threatened, the Hiding Hound puts up or seeks out barriers to hide behind–mental, emotional, or physical withdrawal. The silent treatment and walking out are two common behaviors. Hiding Hounds may be punitive and vindictive. This hound withdraws, but from his protected position he seeks to punish the other person. He withholds information, or betrays, gossips, slanders, and baits his opponent. His goal is to stay hidden and protected while injuring the other.

BITING BULLDOG: She bites, snarls, and openly attacks her opponent. Yelling, accusing, swearing, screaming, berating, and belittling are common behaviors. Biting Bulldogs do not hesitate to go for the jugular. An attack bulldog walks around looking for a fight. She is the instigator. She strikes first. A defensive bulldog does not normally bite unless someone bites her first. But if bitten, she fiercely retaliates. Dog fighting does little or nothing to resolve issues. In fact, it often escalates the conflict.

Day Two

Lay Tracks of Faithfulness

... with ties of loyalty, commitment, and devotion.

"He who is faithful in what is least is faithful also in much; and he who is unjust in what is least is unjust also in much."
Luke 16:10,
New King
James Version

In A.D. 79, Pompeii was destroyed by the eruption of Mount Vesuvius. When archeologists uncovered the site, they found many people buried in the ruins. Most were found in rooms or cellars where they had run to hide. But the Roman sentinel was found standing at the city gate where he had been placed by the captain, his hands still grasping his weapon. While the earth shook beneath him, while people all around fled for shelter, and while floods of volcanic ashes and cinders rained down upon him, he stood faithfully at his post and remained there for more than 1800 years.

In today's lesson we will examine the characteristics of an unfaithful and a faithful person. As you study, ask God to cultivate the qualities of faithfulness in your heart.

Unfaithfulness

In Psalm 101, King David was looking for faithful people to bring into his service. One of the ways he judged the faithfulness of a person's heart was by observing what that person did with his mouth.

Read Psalm 101:3-7. According to verse 5, what does an unfaithful person do with his or her mouth? Write the word in the margin.

Slander, a mark of unfaithfulness, is speech that attacks and injures the reputation of another person. Slander is one of the main types of unfaithful speech and certainly the most damaging, but it is not the only type. In Psalm 101:5, the key word that characterizes unfaithful speech is not *slander,* but *secret.*

Our speech is unfaithful when we say in secret what we would (or should) be ashamed to say in the open with the other person present. Some types of unfaithful speech are:
- slander (Eph. 4:31)
- gossip (Rom. 1:29)
- whispering (see Ps. 41:7)
- talebearing (see Lev. 19:16)
- babbling/chattering (see Prov. 10:8; Eccl. 10:11)
- tattling (see 1 Tim. 5:13)
- defaming (see Jer. 20:10; 1 Cor. 4:13)
- repeating matters (see Prov. 17:9)
- meddling (see Prov. 26:17; 1 Tim. 5:13)

Match these results of unfaithfulness with the correct verses:

Proverbs 10:12	"separates close friends"
Proverbs 17:9	betrays a confidence and tarnishes a reputation
Proverbs 25:9-10	heats up quarrels and kindles strife
Proverbs 25:18	"stirs up dissension"
Proverbs 26:20-21	"like a club or a sword or a sharp arrow"

The problem is not only with those who speak unfaithfully but with those who listen to this type of speech.

Read Proverbs 18:8. According to this verse, listening to unfaithful speech is like:

❑ cutting up a steak   ❑ downing a handful of Smarties
❑ munching on a carrot   ❑ savoring a rare delicacy

"The words of a gossip are like choice morsels; they go down to a man's inmost parts." Proverbs 18:8

The problem with listening to unfaithful speech is that you take it in. You spend time considering it–savoring it. Whether you like it or not, it taints your thoughts and attitudes. Perhaps suspicion and caution arise where previously there were none. Perhaps you begin to see the person spoken of in a slightly different light. Maybe you begin to see faults that you never saw before. As the ancient philosopher Horace said, "Once a word has been allowed to escape, it cannot be recalled."

The story is told of a young man during the Middle Ages who went to a monk to ask what he should do to repent of his sin of slander. The monk instructed the young man to put a feather on every doorstep in town. When the young man returned, the monk instructed him to go back and pick up all the feathers. "But that's impossible," cried the man, "By now the wind will have blown them all over town!"

"So has your slanderous word become impossible to retrieve," replied the monk, "though you are forgiven, you can never retrieve the damage you have done."

When a friend shares his or her opinion or information about someone else, what do you normally do?
❑ savor the information
❑ refuse to listen
❑ direct them to speak to the person they are speaking about
❑ offer a few choice morsels of your own
❑ pass the information on to someone else

Of all our failures in speech, slander and gossip are among the most appalling in God's eyes (see Prov. 6:19). Speaking ill of those in authority and leadership is particularly offensive (see Rom. 13:1-2; 1 Tim. 5:19).[2]

> I would rather play with forked lightning, or take in my hand living wires with their fiery current, than speak a reckless word against any servant of Christ, or idly repeat the slanderous darts which thousands of Christians are hurling on others, to the hurt of their own souls and bodies.
>
> —A.B. Simpson

Unfaithful speech is "detestable" to God because it fractures the unity of His people. It destroys the "body" of Christ (Eph. 5:29-30).

I am saddened by how often Christians gossip and slander and justify doing so in the name of "counseling" or "sharing prayer requests." I am especially disturbed when I hear wives sarcastically slander and demean their husbands. Ladies, when you speak poorly of your husband, you are being unfaithful to him. You are breaking faith.

When we slander and gossip, we are unfaithful to our friends and family. Even more grievous than that, we are unfaithful to God. We "forget" and dishonor Him. Read today's Word from the Word.

[Talebearing] Gab, Blab, and Gossip

I once saw an advertisement that enticed people to buy a cell phone so they could engage in "gab, blab, and gossip." Talebearing is "evil speaking" and includes gossip, slander, defamation, and deceit. It can by done by spreading false reports or by reporting truth maliciously (see Lev. 19:16; Prov. 26:20).

All talebearing is condemned, whether the tales are false (see Matt. 5:11), true (see Prov. 17:9), malicious (see Ps. 31:13), or merely foolish (see Prov. 10:18). Women, in particular, are warned to avoid bearing and listening to tales (see 1 Tim. 3:11; Titus 2:3).

The Bible says talebearing does not build strong relationships. It tears them down (see Prov. 26:20-21) and breaks faith with our friends and with God (see Ps. 15:1,3). Those who are wise will avoid it. Refuse to gab, blab, and gossip.

Read Psalm 50:19-22. According to verse 22, what do those who slander forget? Write your answer in the margin.

Faithfulness

Faithfulness is a huge part of what it means to have unfailing love. *Faithful* means being worthy of confidence, sure, firm, certain, and reliable. A faithful person is loyal, committed, and devoted. Not only does the Bible expect us to be faithful in our relationship to God, it also expects us to be faithful in our relationships with one another.

Read Proverbs 3:3. In the box, draw a picture that describes the instructions in this verse.

"Let love and faithfulness never leave you; bind them around your neck, write them on the tablet of your heart."
Proverbs 3:3

Unfaithfulness is "like a bad tooth or a lame foot" (Prov. 25:19). It inflicts pain and hinders people from functioning well. Faithfulness, on the other hand, is like "the coolness of snow at harvest time," for it brings healing and "refreshes" the hearts of the weary (Prov. 25:13).

God is faithful to us, and we, in turn, can be loyal, committed, and devoted towards others. Though troubles come and all others run away, like the Roman sentinel at Pompeii, we can stand beside our friends faithfully and never abandon our post.

Have you been unfaithful to anyone? Close with a prayer of repentance and commitment to bind faithfulness around your neck and write it on the tablet of your heart.

"Be devoted to one another in brotherly love. Honor one another above yourselves."
Romans 12:10

Conflict Chain

Conflicts left unresolved repeatedly resurface in relationships. If you go through the same conflict pattern whenever a particular issue arises, you are caught in a conflict chain. You can tell if you are caught in a conflict chain if you see a conflict coming and think, "Oh no, not this again!" Child discipline, in-laws, entertainment, sex, money, housework–a conflict chain can be fastened to any subject.

The **trigger** is the event that starts a chain reaction of conflict. For example, Daphne and David are locked into a conflict chain. The chain is triggered whenever Daphne can't balance her checkbook or a check bounces because David has drawn on the account without telling her. The **response** is the sequence of events that occurs after the conflict chain has been triggered. The links in the chain are predictable. David's spending triggers Daphne's anger, which leads to David's defensiveness, which leads to Daphne's apology and concession. The **outcome** is that the issue is never satisfactorily resolved. Daphne and David reach an uneasy truce until the issue surfaces again.

Can you identify any conflict chains in your relationships? To stop the habitual sequence of events, identify the subject, trigger, response, and outcome of your conflict chain. Rehearse a new response. Echo and inquire. Think of a fair forecast you can apply. Don't get drawn into the dogfight.

To close the door on conflict, you have four choices: (1) **Concede**–the needs of one are met. This may be your most godly response.
(2) **Compete**–the stronger party conquers the weaker.
(3) **Converge**–negotiate a treaty or contract. Neither party may be totally satisfied. (4) **Cooperate**–find a "win-win" situation where both parties' needs are met. This may require a creative response.

Day Three

Lay Tracks of Honesty

... with ties of openheartedness, authenticity, and truth.

"Do not lie to each other, since you have taken off your old self with its practices."
Colossians 3:9

One of Norman Rockwell's *Saturday Evening Post* paintings shows an elderly woman buying a large Thanksgiving turkey. The butcher is standing behind the counter weighing the turkey on his scale. Both the butcher and the customer on the other side of the counter are eyeing the scale with pleased expressions on their faces.

Upon closer examination, we discover the reason for their self-satisfaction. The butcher is pressing down on the scale with a thumb to increase the registered weight of the turkey, while the woman is pushing up with a finger to decrease it. Both are oblivious to the other's deception.

This week we will look at the consequences of dishonesty in an effort to build on the foundation of truth in our relationships.

Dishonesty

Ancient weights were stones with flat bases that were carried in a pouch or wallet and used to weigh trade goods. Their weight was to adhere to the standards set by the merchants (see Gen. 23:16). However, in order to deceive and take advantage of others, some carried two differing sets of weights—one for selling and one for buying.

Read Proverbs 20:23. How does God feel about dishonesty?

_____

Duplicity means being *two-faced* or *double*. The dictionary defines it as the practice of "speaking or acting in different ways in relation to the same matter with the intent to deceive." In essence, duplicity is dishonesty. It is like using a false set of weights. The people of Israel were warned against this practice (see Deut. 25:13-15). They were to deal with one another honestly by using honest scales and accurate weights (see Prov. 11:1).

Dishonesty is anything that misleads or conceals truth. It is more than telling lies. Those who don't tell lies can still be dishonest. Honesty involves being openhearted, authentic, and truthful in all our dealings with others. If I am honest, I do not lead people to draw the wrong conclusions about who I am or what I mean. I say what I mean and mean what I say. I am transparent and real—the Bible's description for this is "without guile." Find out more about *guile* by reading today's Word from the Word.

[guile] Hanging Out the Bait

The Greek word translated *guile* means a bait for fish. Like a fisherman baits fish, those with guile bait others with their words. They conceal their true thoughts and intentions while trying to catch others on their *hooks*.

When Jesus saw Nathaniel coming toward Him, He exclaimed, "Here is a true Israelite, in whom there is nothing false [guile]" (John 1:47). In contrast to Jacob, who deceived and tricked his brother out of his birthright (see Gen. 27:35), Nathaniel was an open book. There was no pretension or deception in his spirit. He thought what he said and said what he thought.

Jesus appreciated Nathaniel's candor. Nathaniel was a man worthy of the blessing pronounced in Psalm 32:2: "Blessed is the man ... in whose spirit is no deceit [guile]."

Check the types of dishonesty you have observed. Underline those you would like to eliminate from your speech.

- ❑ misleading
- ❑ exaggerating
- ❑ obscuring
- ❑ fabricating
- ❑ fibbing
- ❑ misrepresenting
- ❑ twisting
- ❑ concealing
- ❑ bluffing
- ❑ subverting
- ❑ distorting
- ❑ downplaying
- ❑ disguising
- ❑ pretending

Dishonest speech creates barriers in relationships because it conceals a person's true thoughts. Dishonesty is a "hiding place" for the unrighteous (Isa. 28:15). When people are dishonest, others have a hard time seeing past the facade. They don't know where the other person is coming from. The words obscure rather than reveal.

People listening to dishonest speech are not entirely certain what the message means–where it comes from and where it is leading. The meaning is not clear, apparent, or true to what is in the person's heart. For example, people can feign friendship while gathering slander in their hearts (see Ps. 41:6). They can say one thing but in their hearts mean something entirely different (see Matt. 5:37). They can wrap their insults and critical barbs in the form of humor and, when confronted, claim "I was only joking" (see Prov. 26:18-19).

Isaiah 41:29 describes dishonesty. To what does it compare dishonest words? Circle the image.

"See, they are all false! Their deeds amount to nothing; their images are but wind and confusion." Isaiah 41:29

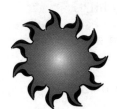   

Have you ever questioned whether others are being truthful with you? Have you wondered whether they are revealing who they really are and what they really think? Or, do you suspect that they are misleading you with words of "wind and confusion"? We often suspect duplicity in others but seldom notice it in ourselves. Many of us see no harm in telling a "little white lie," concealing part of the truth, or sending mixed messages.

Honesty

Read Proverbs 12:17-23. Based on verses 20-23, why should we be honest in our dealings with one another?

_____

_____

The Bible says "an honest answer is like a kiss on the lips" (Prov. 24:26). Honesty is a mark of love. If we are not openhearted, authentic, and truthful with others, we do not love them as we should. The Lord wants us to be honest with one another. He detests dishonest lips but delights in people who are truthful.

> I hope I shall always possess firmness and virtue enough to maintain what I consider the most enviable of all titles, the character of an honest man.
> —George Washington

Honesty must be tempered with prudence. It is inappropriate to tell everybody the truth about what we are thinking. Indiscriminate revelation of our thoughts can be hurtful. Honesty does not mean being open with everybody about everything. But it does mean that we do not mislead. It means that the words we choose accurately represent truth and what is in our hearts "without guile."

The Bible says that "the heart of the righteous weighs its answers" (Prov. 15:28). What do they use to weigh them?

"Honest scales and balances are from the Lord; all the weights in the bag are of his making."
Proverbs 16:11

Read Proverbs 16:11. Who provides "honest scales and balances"? Underline your answer in the margin.

The righteous weigh their words on scales and balances that are from the Lord and with weights that "are of his making." Our words are honest when they line up with God's standards. Are you careful to make sure that all your words are honest and truthful?

In Matthew 5:37, Jesus urged the disciples to be honest in their speech. He told them to "let their 'Yes' be 'Yes,' and your 'No,' 'No'; anything beyond this" is unrighteous. Honest speech is transparent—not laced with multiple meanings,concealing hidden agendas, nor hiding the attitudes of our hearts. It is truthful and authentic.

"Thank you for the gift," the woman gushed, "It's nice to receive something from you that I like." Should the recipient of this sort of compliment be flattered or angry? Did the speaker mean to say that she truly appreciated the gift or that the person giving was inept and had never before given a gift that she appreciated? The meaning is unclear. I suspect that determining her true meaning may have been like trying to nail down the wind.

Dishonest speech keeps people apart. Honest speech lays down tracks of love that help us truly connect with others. Our Tongue Tonics have instructed us how to avoid sending mixed messages and how to promote clarity by using questions and statements in the right way. These techniques are very helpful, but ultimately honest, open speech comes from an honest, open heart.

How honest are you? If you are like me, you have a long way to go to become completely honest in your interactions with others. In examining my heart, I feel very much like David, who said, "I know my transgressions, and my sin is always before me" (Ps. 51:3). David had an acute awareness of his own short fallings. He also had an unshakable confidence in the abundant grace of God to transform his heart. Close today's lesson by joining me in praying David's prayer in the margin.

"Surely you desire truth in the inner parts; you teach me wisdom in the inmost place. Cleanse me with hyssop, and I will be clean; wash me, and I will be whiter than snow … . Create in me a pure heart, O God, and renew a steadfast spirit within me." Psalm 51:6-7,10

Being honest with others involves revealing our true feelings. Today's Tongue Tonic will help you take ownership of your feelings and identify the crux of conflicts.

It's Your Problem

When addressing a problem, identify that you own it. Here is an example: "I have a problem. (Identify Ownership.) You have spent every evening this week playing computer games. (Report.) You seem more interested in playing computer games than in spending time with me. (Analyze.) I miss you. I would like us to spend more time doing things together and relating to each other. (Personalize.) What are some things that you would like to do that I could do with you?" (Nondefensive question.)

By clearly telling others "I have a problem," you greatly decrease the likelihood that they will respond defensively and greatly increase the likelihood that you will resolve your concern constructively.

Have you ever thought, "That was a pointless argument?" Often people argue without really identifying the point–**the crux**–of the conflict. Getting to the crux helps resolve the conflict and lessens the likelihood that a habitual Conflict Chain will form. If the crux is properly identified, both parties will agree with a summary statement such as, "We are at odds about …" or "We differ in …" Objectifying the crux in this way provides clarity and direction for resolving the conflict.

Day Four

Lay Tracks of Tenderheartedness
… with ties of kindness, compassion, and forgiveness.

"Be kind and compassionate to one another, forgiving each other, just as in Christ God forgave you."
Ephesians 4:32

Last week, I filled my freezer to the brim with almost 500 pounds of beef. A friend who raises cattle on a hobby farm had slaughtered a steer and sold us half the meat. Prior to cutting it, the butcher let the carcass hang for two weeks. Apparently, as it hangs, the pull of gravity exerts pressure and the meat becomes more tender. Even so, many of the cuts will have to be specially prepared and cooked to compensate for their natural tendency towards toughness.

No one wants to eat a tough roast or steak. Much of the meat you get from a cow is just that. That's why researchers are testing a new technology to tenderize meat. Hydrodyne technology involves encasing meat in water and pressure-resistant wrapping and submerging it in a massive, steel-domed canister. An explosive charge is set off in the water about 2 feet from the meat. This creates pressures as high as 25,000 pounds per square inch. The technique boasts a 50 to 70 percent improvement in tenderness. With Hydrodyne pressure, even the toughest cut of meat becomes tender, tasty, and enjoyable.[3]

In today's lesson we will confront our choice to respond to the sins and failures of others by becoming hard-hearted or more tenderhearted. By responding in a negative manner, we become calloused and experience distance and alienation. By reacting in a positive manner—with kindness, compassion, and forgiveness—our tender hearts lay down tracks of love that help us connect.

Hard-Hearted

Read Zechariah 7:9-12. In verses 9 and 10, the Lord directed the people of Israel to build tracks of love. He told them to be just, merciful, and compassionate with one another. He commanded them to act with kindness—particularly towards the needy. He also warned them to avoid thinking ill of one another.

According to verse 12, how did the people respond to these instructions?
❑ They eagerly laid ties of kindness and compassion.
❑ They became tenderhearted toward one another.
❑ They rebelled and "made their hearts as hard as flint."
❑ They printed a hard copy and filed it away.

In the New Testament, believers are repeatedly warned against making the same mistake as the people of Israel. "Today, if you hear

108

his voice, do not harden your hearts" (Heb. 3:8,15; 4:9). Hard-heartedness usually shows up when we experience conflict in relationships. It results in wrong attitudes, actions, and words. Some of the sins that characterize hard-heartedness are self-righteousness, conceit, scoffing, malice, threats, gossip, slander, the desire to control and influence others, and vengeance (violence) towards one's opponents (see Ps. 73:6-11).

Ephesians 4:31-32 outlines a hard-hearted and tenderhearted response to the failures of others. Fill in the chart:

Hard-hearted Response: things we should get rid of (v. 31)	Tenderhearted Response: things we should become and do (v. 32)

When we are hard-hearted, we respond to injury or offense with:

bitterness	ill feelings	We harbor resentment and have a "bad taste" in our spirits. We feel injured and assaulted.
rage and anger	ill thoughts	Our thoughts and assumptions about that person emotionally inflame us. We mentally rehash the situation and become increasingly agitated.
brawling and slander	ill speech	We have difficulty speaking to the person civilly (brawling). When we speak about her to others, we have nothing good to say (slander).
forms of malice	ill intentions	We wish evil upon the person who hurt us. We desire revenge, plot revenge, and get revenge. We rejoice in her downfall and gloat over her misfortune. We want to see her fail, see her punished, and see her suffer.

I don't know about you, but my first tendency when wounded is to "harden" and not to "soften." But the consequence of becoming calloused toward another person is much broader than that one relationship. Callousness of heart severely affects my relationship with God. If I don't work at being tender toward the person who has wounded me, I hamper my ability to be tender toward God. I begin to "miss" the grace of God. The bitter root in my heart grows bigger, my attitude causes trouble, and many people and relationships are defiled (see Heb. 12:15).

Tenderhearted

How do we keep our hearts tender? Colossians 3:12-14 mentions eight items that we need to keep in our wardrobe. List them on the pieces of clothing. (Check the footnote for help.)[4]

Think of a challenging relationship in which you are involved. Is your heart tender? Take a personal inventory to see if you have "clothed" yourself properly. Check off the attitudes that apply to you:

TENDERHEARTED
❏ I am compassionate. I have a merciful, charitable spirit.
❏ I am patient. I do not react when provoked.
❏ I am kind. I am friendly, pleasant, and good-natured.
❏ I am forgiving as the Lord forgives me. I will be quick to ask for forgiveness.
❏ I am humble. I recognize my own fallibility. I do not insist on my own way.
❏ I am loving. I value you highly. I will love you sacrificially.
❏ I am gentle. My words are gracious and amiable.

HARD-HEARTED
❏ I am filled with bad feelings, resentment and malice. I am concerned about how you injured me, not how I serve you.
❏ I am cruel. I try to avoid you or hurt you.
❏ I hold grudges. I have a right to make you pay for your sins. I jump to conclusions.
❏ I am self-righteous. I feel better than you because you are wrong, and I am right..
❏ I don't like you. You are unworthy. Unlike me, you are a cruel and terrible person.
❏ I am harsh. My thoughts, words, and actions are cutting and severe.

Were you able to check all the boxes in the tenderhearted column? Probably not. We are like tough cuts of meat–tenderness goes against our natural tendencies. But through the power of the Holy Spirit, we are able to work towards having increasingly tender hearts.

Tenderizing is a process. Normally, the more deeply we have been hurt by someone, the longer the process of tenderization takes. The important thing is to "keep the pressure on." Hard-heartedness is not something to justify but something to grieve deeply and work against diligently. God wants us to desperately desire a tender heart.

Do you want to have a tender heart toward God? Then pursue a tender heart towards those who hurt you. If you seek, you will find. If you ask, God will answer. If you knock with diligence and desperation, He'll open the door. Through humility, pain, sacrifice, and the deepest of joy, you will lay ties that build tracks of love.

We win by tenderness; we conquer by forgiveness.
—Fredrick William Robertson

Close today's lesson by reading Ezekiel 36:26-36. Repent of your hardness of heart and meditate on God's promise to you.

Resolve Conflict

Conflict is inevitable. If you manage conflict poorly, your relationships will suffer. If you manage conflict well, your relationships will grow healthy and strong. Here are some steps to resolve conflict:

REMAIN CALM: Rash, uncontrolled speech is damaging speech. Once spoken, words can never be retracted. Ask God to give you the power to remain calm during conflict and to think before you speak.

ECHO AND INQUIRE: Make sure you understand the other person's meaning and motivation. Most conflicts escalate because we jump to conclusions without checking to see if our perception is accurate. Take your time. There will be plenty of opportunity to respond after you understand. Remember, understanding does not equal assent. Listen with humble, open ears. Make it your aim for the other person to be satisfied that you understand what they want.

STATE YOUR POSITION: Be personal, honest, and direct. Then inquire to find out how the other person is interpreting your message.

OBJECTIFY THE CRUX: Is the conflict about facts, how to proceed, differing goals, or principle? Objectify the crux of the conflict with a summary statement: "It seems that we are at odds about … "

LIST ALTERNATIVES: Ask, "What are some ways we can address both of our concerns?" or "What do you think we should do about this situation?" Be creative. Try to identify several options.

VALIDATE NEEDS: Choose the solution that validates the needs of both parties–the "win-win" scenario. Remember, the worst way to close a conflict is to remain deadlocked in competition. The best way to close it is to cooperate.

ESTABLISH A PLAN: Follow through on it. Support the decision with your attitude as well as your actions.

Day Five

Lay Tracks of Discretion

... with ties of discernment, prudence, and good judgment.

This week's lessons have focused on helping you build relationships by filling your speech with nourishment, faithfulness, honesty and tenderheartedness. These qualities are of great worth. They make your words as beautiful and valuable as gold. But one thing remains in order to "complete" the picture.

Use Discretion

"A word aptly spoken is like apples of gold in settings of silver."
Proverbs 25:11

Read Proverbs 25:11. The gold apple needs to be showcased in an appropriate frame—a "setting" of silver. What is the silver setting that showcases golden words?
❑ speaking aptly (fitly)
❑ speaking behind a podium
❑ speaking through a megaphone
❑ speaking on television

Apt means suitable, appropriate, fitting. When we speak aptly, we speak with discretion. Our words are discerning, prudent, and show good judgment. We not only know what to say, but also we know how and when to say it. How often have you "stuck your foot in your mouth" by saying something in the wrong way or at the wrong time? Often it is the delivery and timing of our message that is inappropriate, not the words themselves. The apple is fine, but the frame is bent out of shape.

Proverbs 11:22 says that "a beautiful woman" without discretion is "like a gold ring in a pig's snout." You can have the most beautiful words, but if you have no discretion, the whole effect is spoiled.

Read the following verses. Beside each reference, record how the people lacked discretion:

Proverbs 19:19 _____

Proverbs 23:9 _____

Ephesians 5:4_____

The wise heart is not indiscriminate. It knows when to "overlook an insult" (Prov. 12:16) and when to rebuke sin (see 1 Tim. 5:20). It knows when to keep "knowledge to himself" (Prov. 12:23) and when to share it with others (see Prov. 9:9). It knows when to "heed correction" (Prov. 15:5) and when to ignore opinions (see Prov. 26:6-9). It knows when to pick someone up and when to let him or her fall down (see Prov. 19:19). It knows when to draw closer (see Prov. 27:9-10) and when to run and "take refuge" (Prov. 22:3).

According to Solomon, "the wise heart will know the proper time and procedure" for every matter (Eccl. 8:5), and wise lips will know the fitting thing to say (see Prov. 10:32). I wish I always knew the proper time, procedure, and most fitting thing to say! I often say things I shouldn't say. More often, I don't say things I should. Even when my heart is right, I can lack discretion and fail miserably.

"Preserve sound judgment and discernment, do not let them out of your sight; they will be life for you, an ornament to grace your neck."
Proverbs 3:21-22

Build Each Other Up

How can we make sure our words are fitting? Our Breath Freshener for the week, Ephesians 4:29, provides some counsel. Reread it on page 94. Underline the words *helpful for building others*, *their needs*, and *benefit*.

These phrases help us judge the appropriateness of our words. Our words are fitting when they are helpful for building others up, when they are focused on the other person's needs and not merely our own, and when they benefit the other person. As we saw in this week's Talk Show, the word *benefit* is the word *charis* from which we also get the word *grace*. Words are of "benefit" when they carry God's grace–the force of His love–into the lives of others.

What we must ask ourselves, therefore, when discerning the aptness of our words, is not only "Is it right?" but also, "Will it be helpful for building the person up? Is it what he or she needs? Is it the right time?" and, "Is it full of grace?" A wise person asks these questions and seeks the Holy Spirit's counsel.

A husband and wife quarreled. In frustration the wife grabbed two sheets of paper and said

Wisdom is the right use of knowledge. To know is not to be wise. Many men know a great deal, and are all the greater fools for it. There is no fool so great a fool as the knowing fool. But to know how to use knowledge is to have wisdom.
—Charles Spurgeon

to her husband, "Let's list our grievances by writing down each other's faults." The woman started writing. The man watched her for a few moments and then wrote on his paper. She wrote again. He watched her, and every time she stopped, he would write again. They finished and exchanged papers. When she saw what he had written, she began to cry. She had listed his many faults. But line after line, he had merely written down, "I love you, I love you, I love you."

Which words focused on the other's needs instead of personal needs? Which words were the most helpful for building up? Which words were full of grace? The point of this illustration is not that our words ought to never contain rebuke or correction. At times, they most certainly must. Correction can sting and wound. But even in rebuke our words ought—in humility and brokenness of spirit—to focus on what is helpful for building the other person up, on his or her needs, and on what will best transport God's grace.

How does Proverbs 15:23 describe a timely word?
❏ difficult   ❏ good
❏ welcomed   ❏ well-received

A timely word may not be welcomed or well-received. It may or may

> Being all fashioned of the self-same dust, Let us be merciful as well as just.
> —Henry Wadsworth Longfellow

not be a difficult word, but it is definitely a good word. For that reason, there is joy in store for the one who speaks it. Sound judgment and discernment help us to know how to speak the right word in the right season. "Like apples of gold in settings of silver," our words can be nourishing, faithful, appropriate, honest, and tender-hearted.

To build tracks of love, we are desperately dependent on the constant guidance of the Holy Spirit. As we rely on Him to help us lay down good ties, we will see lines built, connect with one another, and experience increased harmony and unity in our relationships. That's the power of construction!

Look back over this week's lessons. What did God teach you this week, and how can you apply what you have learned?

_____

_____

This week's Tongue Tonics provided practical tools to help you manage conflict constructively. Conflict is a prime opportunity to speak nourishing, faithful, honest, tenderhearted, and discerning words.

[1] As quoted in *Illustrations for Biblical Preaching*, Michael P. Green, ed., (Grand Rapids, MI: Baker Book House, 1989), 119.
[2] By necessity, leaders must discuss what the rest of us are not free to discuss. Faithfulness to God requires that they share information and make decisions to nurture, direct, and correct people under their authority. But this freedom comes with an awesome responsibility. Their speech will be judged even more severely than those who are not in leadership roles (see Jas. 3:1).
[3] Jill Lee, "Big Shock Makes Tender Beef," *ARS News & Information*, http.//www.ars.usda.gov/is/pr/1998/980629.htm, Jan. 23, 2001.
[4] Compassion, kindness, humility, gentleness, patience, forbearance (bear with), forgiveness, and love.

Bypass the Bait

When someone throws an inflammatory or critical comment our way, it's tempting to take the bait and get into an argument or internally bristle at what he or she said. A better way to handle the situation is to bypass the bait. Remember to remain calm and to echo and inquire. The quickest way to neutralize a critic is to agree with him or her. Agree with the part that is valid or with the critic's right to an opinion. You don't need to agree with the entire assessment; just find a part that you can agree with. At the very least, you can agree that they have the right to think the way they do.

If appropriate, follow up your agreement with a quick statement in which you disclose your opinion or intent. If you are able to remain calm and neutral through this process, chances are you will neutralize the comment and prevent it from developing into an argument. This technique is particularly helpful when you are dealing with people with a grumpy disposition who make inflammatory, opinionated, off-the-cuff comments and have no particular issue to resolve.

Here's how it works:
Steven snaps at Chris: "This casserole tastes awful! Can't you find any better recipes?"
Chris: "What do you mean by awful?" (Nondefensive question)
Steven: "I mean it's bland and tasteless!"
Chris: "You like your food to have more flavor." (Echo.) "I can see why you might not enjoy this meal." (Agrees with his right to an opinion.) "I always enjoy trying recipes I haven't tried before." (Disclose.)

Resist Manipulation

Sometimes, people will try to get you to do things you don't want to do by badgering and manipulating you. They might give you lots of reasons, ridicule, beg, or accuse you. They hope that if they try hard enough and long enough, they will wear you down and convince you to give in. Here's a simple technique to use after you are sure you understand the other person's position and have made your own position clear.
BUFFER: Buffer yourself against manipulation. Don't let the comments "stick." Let them run off like water off a duck's back.
AGREE: Agree with the comment (in whole or in part), or agree with the person's right to an opinion. "I can see why you might think that…"
REWIND/REPEAT: Rewind the tape and repeat your position.

Jane: "Would you like to baby-sit tonight?"
Karen: "No. I am tired and want to spend a quiet evening at home tonight."
Jane: "I don't know if I can find another sitter on such short notice."
Karen: "That may be, but I just want to spend a quiet evening at home tonight."
Jane: (getting agitated) "I really need to get out! Don't you care?"
Karen: "I can see that you want to go out tonight and I do care, but I am tired and want to spend a quiet evening at home."
Jane: "Some friend you are!"
Karen: "I can see how you might feel irritated with me, but I just want to spend a quiet evening at home tonight. Ask me again some other time."

The Power of Instruction
Speech transformation is a lifelong process.

Week Six

Over the past weeks you have put some new communication skills into practice. Perhaps, like me, you have also discovered that you have much more to learn. In this final week of lessons, harness the power of instruction and commit to the lifelong process of speech transformation.

Speech Arts? It's an unconventional program that accepts unlikely candidates, gives them a unique guarantee, and achieves uncommon results! In this week's Talk Show, you'll discover the program that guarantees a gold medal in speech.

Day 1: Speech Reform School
   The need for an instructed tongue
Day 2: Apprenticeship Program
   The model for an instructed tongue
Day 3: The Love of Learning
   The desire for an instructed tongue
Day 4: A Teachable Spirit
   The discipline of an instructed tongue
Day 5: Highest Honors
   The triumph of an instructed tongue

This Week's Tongue Tonics:
   • Degrees of Disclosure
   • Relationship Bank Balance
   • Communication Climate
   • Relationsbip Spirals
   • Saying "I'm Sorry"

   • A Sorry "Sorry"
   • Ace Your Appreciation
   • Constructive Feedback
   • Get Connected
   • Stay Committed

"The Sovereign Lord has given me an instructed tongue, to know the word that sustains the weary. He wakens me morning by morning, wakens my ear to listen like one being taught" (Isa. 50:4).

Cut out the Scripture card on page 147 as a memory tool.

The Power of Instruction: God's School of Speech Arts
Isaiah 6:5-8; 50:4; 51:16; 59:21

This Talk Show guide will help you follow the video for Session Six.

1. God enrolls unlikely candidates.

    a. Isaiah (see Isa. 6:5)
    b. Jeremiah (see Jer. 1:6)
    c. Ezekiel (see Ezek. 3:14-15)
    d. Daniel (see Dan. 10:15-17)
    e. Disciples (see Mark 3:13-19; 14:29)
    f. Apostle Paul (see Acts 20:9; 1 Cor. 10:10)
    g. Moses (see Ex. 3:11; 4:10; 6:12)

2. God gives a unique guarantee.

    a. His _____ is with us (see Isa. 59:12).

    b. He will put _____ in our mouths (see Isa. 51:16).

    c. He will provide _____ for the tests (see Luke 12:11-12).

3. God's program is unconventional.

    a. He puts His _____ on the students (see Jer. 1:9).

    b. All He asks is that we _____ (see Ps. 81:10; Isa. 50:4-5; Ezek. 3:27).

    c. His program is focused on _____, not product (see Ps. 38:13-15).

4. God's results are uncommon.

    a. Isaiah (see Isa. 50:4-5)
    b. Moses (see Deut. 31:30)

In God's school, you are in your very own category. He doesn't compare you to anyone else. If you are enrolled in His program, all you need to do is listen, stand up, and open your mouth ... and victory will be yours! That's the power of instruction.

Speech Reform School
The need for an instructed tongue

"Not that I have already obtained all this, or have already been made perfect, but I press on to take hold of that for which Christ Jesus took hold of me."
Philippians 3:12

His gloomy look told me immediately that something had gone wrong. He tossed his book bag into the back of our vehicle, crossed his arms, and with a heavy sigh slumped down into the seat next to me. "Hi sweetie," I ventured, "It looks like you've had a hard day."

"I don't understand it," my son burst out bitterly. "I studied, and I thought I knew all the material. How could I blow a test so badly? Thirty-seven percent!–I am so disgusted!"

Thirty-seven percent? That's pretty bad. Especially since he is an honor-roll student. But I know the feeling. I've been confident in my preparation, knowledge, and performance–thinking that all was well–only to be confronted with the fact that I had totally blown it. I know that sick feeling that washes over your insides when you suddenly become conscious of your own shortcomings.

We Are Imperfect

The prophet Isaiah was also familiar with that feeling of imperfection. When we first meet him in chapters 1 through 5 of the Book of Isaiah, he confidently proclaimed his visions and the judgment of God on the people's sins. Chapter 5 shows him pronouncing "woes" on all the failures of his fellow Israelites:

"Woe to those who draw sin along with cords of deceit, and wickedness as with cart ropes" (v. 18). "Woe to those who call evil good and good evil, who put darkness for light and light for darkness, who put bitter for sweet and sweet for bitter. Woe to those who are wise in their own eyes and clever in their own sight" (vv. 20-21).

But in chapter 6, Isaiah hits the wall. He is confronted with a vision of the holiness of God and becomes acutely aware of his own shortcomings.

Read Isaiah 6:1-8. In verse 5, Isaiah no longer cries out "Woe to you" or "Woe to those" as he did in the previous chapter. What does he cry out?

_____

Woe is an expression of grief and sorrow. It conveys a feeling of misery and extreme wretchedness. When Isaiah saw the failure of the people of Israel he condemned them by saying, "Woe to you!" But when he was confronted with the glory of God, he saw that he had also failed the test–and that sick feeling washed over him. In bitter misery, he cried out, "Woe is me!"

Isaiah, the prophet who had been transmitting the holy words of God, was overcome with grief and sorrow at the "unclean" condition of his own mouth. When confronted with "the Word," he saw that his own words did not even come close to making the grade.

My son Matthew plays football. Almost every day during football season he dons his white football pants and joins his team for practice (White practice pants! Go figure!) They practice "rain or shine," and near the end of the season, even in the snow.

Every week Matt brings his pants and socks home to be washed. As you can well imagine, getting out the ground-in mud and grass is the challenge laundry commercials are made of. I soak and scrub, and scrub and soak. When it comes time for equipment return, I work particularly hard at getting them spotlessly clean. I am determined to hand-in practice pants that are still white. (White! I'll never understand!)

At the end of last season, Matt's practice pants looked great compared to the pants of many of the other boys. But there is "white" and then there is "WHITE!" If you were to put a brand-new pair of football pants beside the ones I was so proud of cleaning, you would see that my "white" was tragically gray and dirty in comparison.

Compared to the people around him, Isaiah's life looked "white." But compared to the dazzling holiness of God, he was filthy. If you compare yourself to the braggart down the street, or the foul-mouthed supervisor in your office, or to your own past habits, you may give yourself an average or even a good mark. But what would your mark be if you, like Isaiah, compared yourself to the holiness of God?

This is the very perfection of a man, to find out his own imperfection.
—Augustine

Compared to God's, my speech deserves a grade of _____.

God is so holy, that the "goodness" of our speech wouldn't even register on the lowest end of the scale. No wonder Isaiah was overwhelmed! I felt the same way as I wrote this study. When I began to write, God showed me a glimpse of the glory and flawlessness of His words–and I became overwhelmed at my filthy mouth.

Match the following verses to the summaries of how they describe God's speech:

Psalm 12:6	Perfect, flawless
Psalm 18:30	Flawless, pure
Psalm 19:7-10	Unbounded, limitless perfection
Psalm 119:96	Trustworthy, right, radiant

We Are Being Made Perfect

"Wait!" you could protest: "God is perfect, but humans aren't perfect! Why should I compare myself to His perfect standard? I do much better when I compare myself to the norm of humanity." That's a very good question. Why should we compare our speech to God's standard of perfection?

Write Hebrews 10:14 in your own words.

_____

_____

Because of His sacrifice for those who trust in Him, Jesus Christ has made us perfect forever. By virtue of our acceptance of Him, we are already perfect. That's *justification.* The second part of the verse says that we are being made perfect. There is a process going on in us that makes us more holy and less sinful. That's *sanctification.* (If you want to review the meanings of these words, take a look back to the Word from the Word in week 2, day 1, p. 32.)

To deny that we could ever achieve perfection is to deny the reality of the presence of God's Spirit in us. We are expected to push for His standard of perfection because He is perfect and He lives in us. Jesus commanded us to "Be perfect, therefore, as your heavenly

We conquer—not in any brilliant fashion—we conquer by continuing.
—George Matheson

Father is perfect" (Matt. 5:48). That's why the apostles struggled so hard to "present everyone perfect in Christ" (Col 1:28). And that's why in our speech, we can and ought to "aim for perfection" (2 Cor. 13:11) and compare ourselves only to God's standard of perfection.

Read Philippians 3:12–4:1. In verses 13-14, what one thing was Paul committed to do for the rest of his life?

_____

Paul knew that the process of being "made perfect" would not be completed until he got to heaven. But he was determined to press on toward that goal.

As Isaiah discovered, we all fall short of God's perfection, particularly when it comes to our speech. We are all–even the best of us–candidates for lifelong speech reform.

Close today's lesson by making the commitment to stay enrolled in God's School of Speech Arts for the rest of your life. Ask Him for the desire and ability to help you "press on" to reach the goal of perfect speech.

Today's Tongue Tonic reminds us that others can help us grow in perfection by our willingness to open ourselves to them. For relationships to grow, we must be willing to invest.

Degrees of Disclosure

The degree to which individuals reveal themselves to one another corresponds to the level of intimacy in their relationship. Superficial relationships require a relatively low degree of self-disclosure, while close, intimate relationships require a high level of disclosure. There are five degrees of disclosure in interpersonal conversation.

Clichés: Clichés are ritualized, stereotyped phrases that are used in social situations. "How are you doing?" "Just Fine." "I'm pleased to meet you." "Good to see you." "Let's get together sometime." "Take care!" These stock phrases are used for surface social interactions. The grocery clerk would be quite surprised and perhaps embarrassed if you responded to her casual "How are you?" with a lengthy discourse on your love life, finances, or health. Clichés are responses requiring the lowest degree of self disclosure. They are non-revealing and non-vulnerable.

Facts, Information, Explanations: People exchange facts or information such as where they were born, which schools they attended, their marital status, whether they have children, or their occupations. Couples might exchange information about work schedules, the children's grades, who needs rides, or whose turn it is to make supper.

Ideas and Opinions: Ideas and opinions reveal more about a person than facts alone. With this third degree of disclosure, people state their likes or dislikes and their opinions on matters. They begin to share their thoughts.

Beliefs, Concerns, Experiences: When people reveal personal beliefs, values, concerns, and significant (life-shaping) experiences, they are conversing at the fourth degree of disclosure. At this level we begin to see more of who they really are. They reveal the foundations and motivating forces that shape their behavior.

Innermost Thoughts and Feelings: At the deepest level, people totally disclose their innermost thoughts and feelings. They share their deepest hopes, fears, struggles, failures, and victories.

In order to deepen our relationships, we must self-disclose at deeper levels. If the other person reciprocates, the relationship will increase in intimacy.

Relationship Bank Balance

Regard your relationships as an account with a bank balance. Each time you interact positively–speaking affirming, encouraging words–you make a deposit into that account. Each time you speak critically or negatively, you make a withdrawal. Is the balance in your account growing? Are you investing in the relationship or accumulating a debt and headed for foreclosure? Does your account have a large enough balance to cover the stress of unexpected events? When it comes to relationships, it's best to invest. In doing so, we lay up the "treasures" of friendship and love that God intended for us.

Day Two

Apprenticeship Program
The model for an instructed tongue

"Hold on to instruction, do not let it go; guard it well, for it is your life."
Proverbs 4:13

Some time ago the famous pianist, Paderewski, arrived early for a performance in a small Connecticut town. He decided to take a walk. He heard a piano being played, and upon following the sound, came to a house that advertised: "Miss Jones. Piano lessons. 25 cents an hour."

Miss Jones was trying to play one of Chopin's nocturnes and was not succeeding very well. Paderewski knocked on the door and inquired if he might not help. Delighted, she invited him in and spent the next hour with the master pianist, listening to him play and having him correct her technique.

Some months later, Paderewski returned to the town. While walking, he came upon the home of Miss Jones and was startled to see that her sign now read: "Miss Jones–Pupil of Paderewski–Piano lessons. $1.00 an hour."

Great teachers produce great students. In today's lesson we'll see that great speech comes from apprenticing under the master speech instructor: Jesus Christ, who is "The Word" sent from God the Father (John 1:14).

Jesus Is Our Teacher

"I will instruct you and teach you in the way you should go; I will counsel you and watch over you."
Psalm 32:8

The teacher-pupil relationship was a common feature in the ancient world. Greek philosophers often mentored groups of apprentices. Socrates mentored Plato, who in turn mentored Aristotle. Eminent Jewish Rabbis also had their own schools for higher learning in which they mentored disciples. Hillel and Shammai are two notable examples of first-century rabbis. Another example is Gamaliel, who had 80 students, one of whom was the apostle Paul (see Acts 22:3).

The word *apprentice* comes from the French word, *aprende:* to learn. An apprentice is one who is put under the care of a skilled master for the purpose of learning a trade or profession. Apprenticeship often involves a legal agreement whereby the master commits to teach and the apprentice commits to learn. Though the Jewish establishment did not officially recognize Jesus as a teacher, He, too, had a group of students who called Him *Rabbi* and *tutor* (Mark 9:5; 11:21; John 3:2).

Read Matthew 11:29. What did Jesus invite people to do?

Jesus invited people to take on His yoke and learn from Him. His "yoke" referred to the process of training a young bullock to plow. To train a bullock, farmers harnessed it to the same yoke as a mature ox. The young bullock, which was dwarfed in size by the large animal, did not pull any of the weight. It merely learned to walk in a field under control, harnessed to a partner. The ox pulled all the weight and set the direction for the youngster, whose only responsibility was to walk alongside.

Jesus invited people to enter into a learning relationship with Him. He, the teacher, was the ox and His students the young bullocks. He promised that those who bound themselves to Him in this apprenticeship would not bear a heavy load. He would bear the load and set direction for them. They would merely need to walk alongside.

In Luke 6:40, what did Jesus say a "fully trained" student would be like?

❑ an egghead   ❑ his teacher

❑ perfect   ❑ well-educated

"A student is not above his teacher, but everyone who is fully trained will be like his teacher." Luke 6:40

Fully trained students become like their teachers. In His invitation to come learn from Him, Jesus described Himself as "gentle and humble in heart" (Matt. 11:29). When fully trained, His apprentices would be just like Him. Because students become like their teachers, Jesus warned people against yoking themselves to arrogant masters.

Read Matthew 23:1-12. Jesus bears the heavy load for His apprentices. According to verse 4, what did the other teachers do for theirs?

_____

Jesus is humble and gentle. According to verses 5-6, what was the other teachers' motivation?

_____

Phylacteries were small boxes or pouches containing copies of certain Scripture verses (see Ex. 13:2-16; Deut. 6:4-9; 11:13-21). These were worn as armbands or headbands. The practice developed as an overly literal application of Deuteronomy 6:8 and 11:18, where the people were instructed to "tie" them (the instructions) as symbols on their hands and bind them on your foreheads."

"Tassels on their garments" refers to the zizith–a Jewish prayer shawl whose fringes were used somewhat like rosary beads to count and keep track of the various prayers that the wearer recited. The rabbis made sure that both their phylacteries and tassels were noticeable. They wanted people to know that they were the teachers.

Why were Christ's disciples not to claim the title (see vv. 8-10):

"Rabbi" ("my great one")? _____

"Father"? _____

"Teacher"? _____

Jesus taught that when leaders claim a higher privilege, status, or greater worth than those they lead, they claim that which does not belong to them. Ultimately, God alone is our Master, our Father, and Christ, our Teacher. Jesus is not arguing against human leadership. But He is arguing against an attitude of arrogance that sets self on a pedestal. Christ's students follow His example of humility, service, and self-sacrifice. When Jesus finished washing His disciples' feet, He asked them: "'Do you understand what I have done for you?' ... 'You call me "Teacher" and "Lord," and rightly so, for that is what I am. Now that I, your Lord and Teacher, have washed your feet, you also should wash one another's feet. I have set you an example that you should do as I have done for you'" (John 13:12-15).

> Knowledge is proud that he has learn'd so much; Wisdom is humble that he knows not more.
> —William Cowper

Jesus Learned from the Father

Jesus is our example of both what it means to be a teacher and what it means to be a student. As a student, Jesus learned from God, His Father (see John 15:15). He learned obedience by doing exactly what His Father commanded (see John 14:31; Heb. 5:7-9). He spoke the Father's words (see John 17:8). He listened to His Father's voice so that He would know exactly what to say and how to say it (see John 14:24).

Jesus is the perfect student because He is exactly like His teacher (see John 14:9). For this reason, the Father designated Jesus to be our teacher (see Heb. 5:1-10). Unlike the other rabbis, this was not a position Jesus self-confidently took upon Himself. He became our teacher out of humble obedience to the Father.

In following Christ, we become good students. We become like Him. Jesus invites people to follow Him. I hope you have made the commitment to do so. But do you realize that a big part of this commitment is learning how to manage your mouth?

"He committed no sin, and no deceit was found in his mouth." When they hurled their insults at him, he did not retaliate; when he suffered, he made no threats.
1 Peter 2:22-23

Read 1 Peter 2:22-23. Underline the words that indicate how Christ used His mouth.

Followers of Christ enter into a lifelong apprenticeship with the master of transformed speech. They bind themselves to the goal of perfection in speech. And they seek to improve their speech on a daily basis (see Luke 9:23). God wants you to work on improving your speech every day for the rest of your life. That's a big part of what it means to be an apprentice of Christ.

Apprentices often enter into formal agreements with their teachers. Christ has promised to be your speech teacher. Have you promised to work on learning to use your mouth properly? If you are serious about your apprenticeship, close today's lesson by praying, indicating your commitment to continually work on your speech.

Communication Climate

The climate of a relationship can be described in weather terms: stormy, cold, cloudy, warm, sunny. The same is true of groups such as a family, church, or workplace. Have you ever been in an environment where criticism, sarcasm, backbiting, and suspicion were predominant? Or have you experienced a positive, supportive, affirming environment? If so, you know what a difference communication climate makes.

The most basic act of positive affirmation is to take note of an individual's presence. **Noticing others** means that we make eye contact, turn our bodies toward and not away from them, approach them, smile, and acknowledge that they are there. Negative communication climates fail in this most basic area. People walk past one another and around one another without indicating that they notice another's presence. They avoid eye contact, do not approach, and appear reluctant to connect. **Affirmation** occurs when people make the effort to engage. Though the degree of self-disclosure may be low, they willingly and eagerly enter into conversation. People feel even more affirmed when others seek to understand their ideas and feelings by asking questions and carefully listening to them. By **acknowledging** them in this way, we communicate that their ideas and feelings are important to us. It is possible to disagree with someone's ideas or feelings but still **endorse** the part with which we agree. Compliments, praise, expressions of gratitude, and public acknowledgement are endorsing behaviors.

If you wish to change a negative communication climate, ask God for the ability to notice, affirm, acknowledge, and endorse those around you.

Relationship Spirals

When Cindy rushed past Jane, Jane assumed that Cindy was rude. So the next time she saw her, Jane turned aside slightly as Cindy approached the group. Cindy assumed Jane did not like her, so she began to avoid her. Whenever they did have occasion to interact, both were defensive and cynical. Jane and Cindy are locked in a negative relationship spiral. In order to break the spiral, one party must be willing to respond in a manner opposite to what they feel they have received. Or, they must be willing to ask questions to clarify their perceptions. If you are in a relationship spiral, ask God to help you break the spiral by responding with kindness and love.

Day Three

The Love of Learning
The desire for an instructed tongue

"I have put my words in your mouth and covered you with the shadow of my hand."
Isaiah 51:16

Do you remember Aesop's fable about the fox and the grapes? A famished fox saw some clusters of plump black grapes hanging from a trellised vine. She tried and tried to reach them, but wearied herself in vain. At last she turned away, hiding her disappointment, and said, "I'm sure those grapes were sour anyway."

When it comes to changing our speech habits, some of us are like that fox. We see the promise of transformed speech, but after a few tries, we decide that the fruit is out of our reach. We walk away and look for something else to fill our hunger.

An Impossible Goal?

The people of Israel suspected that obeying God was out of their reach. Read Deuteronomy 30:11-14. Write what Moses told them in verse 14.

_____

_____

God does not leave His words dangling from a trellis–high and out of reach. No, as we will see in today's lesson, transformed speech is not out of our reach. It is very near. He puts the right words in our mouths and in our hearts. We merely need to come to Him with an appetite and an intense desire to be filled.

God tells His people: "I am the Lord your God. ... Open wide your mouth and I will fill it" (Ps. 81:10). According to an ancient custom, when a benevolent king wished to extend a favor or special honor to a visitor, he would ask him to open wide his mouth. The king would then cram it full of sweetmeats. Occasionally he would even put in a handful of jewels. Our King wants to fill our mouths with the precious jewel of transformed speech. All He asks is that we "open up."

Ezekiel the prophet had a vision (see Ezek. 2:7–3:4). In this vision, God asked the prophet to eat a scroll. On the scroll were words from God, expressing His sorrow about the waywardness of His people. God presented Ezekiel with the scroll and asked him to eat it.

What did God's words taste like? (3:3) _____

After eating God's words, what was Ezekiel asked to do? (v. 4)

My mother always said, "You are what you eat." God's words were sweet as honey in Ezekiel's mouth. When Ezekiel opened his mouth, he was filled with the sweet taste of God's words and was consequently filled with words to speak to others.

Evil words can also taste sweet, but the Bible tells us that they will turn sour in our stomachs. They "will become the venom of serpents within" us (Job. 20:12-14). Those who are evil will desire, crave, and devour evil, but they will not be satisfied. Distress, misery, and vomiting are the end result of filling one's belly with this type of food (see Job 20:21-23).

"You are what you eat." Perhaps we could add to that old adage, "You will be filled with what you desire." King David had an appetite for the right kind of food. He said, "I open my mouth and pant, longing for your commands" (Ps. 119:131). Those

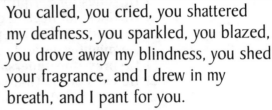

You called, you cried, you shattered my deafness, you sparkled, you blazed, you drove away my blindness, you shed your fragrance, and I drew in my breath, and I pant for you.
—Augustine

who have been filled with the sweetness of God's fare long for it above all else–more than a deer longs for water, more than the earth longs for the sun, more than lungs long for oxygen.

Read Job 23:11-12, Psalm 119:72, and Psalm 119:103. Write each reference under the corresponding picture:

Long for it more than the sweetest pleasures

Long for it more than money

Long for it more than daily needs

Desire Is the Key

Longing to be filled with holy words is essentially longing to be filled with the fullness of Christ, who is "the Word." Your desire for transformed speech is thus an indicator of your longing for God. How badly do you want it? Do you crave being filled and transformed more than you crave the sweetest pleasures, money, and even your daily needs?

Put an "X" on the scale to indicate your level of desire.
I have no desire to be filled. **I am desperate to be filled.**

Your behavior is the best indicator of your desire. The following list describes one who "opens his mouth and pants" for God's Word.

Check the statements about David that characterize yourself:
☐ He respects Scripture (see Ps. 119:162).
☐ He is full of zeal for Scripture (see Ps. 119:139).
☐ He longs for Scripture at all times (see Ps. 119:20).
☐ He does not neglect reading Scripture (Ps. 119:16).
☐ He meditates on Scripture day and night (see Ps. 1:2; 119:97).
☐ He memorizes and recites Scripture (see Ps. 119:11-13).
☐ He prays for understanding daily (see Ps. 119:18,55).
☐ He calls out to God with all his heart (see Ps. 119:10,145).
☐ He obeys and lives according to Scripture (see Ps. 119:8-10).
☐ He grieves when Scripture is not obeyed (see Ps. 119:136).
☐ His speech is filled with the themes of Scripture (see Ps. 119:54).
☐ He practices what he learns from Scripture (see Ps. 119:60).
☐ He finds great joy in speaking the right words
  (see Ps. 119:162-165).
☐ He doesn't follow the speech patterns of those around him
  (see Ps. 119:69).
☐ He responds to hurt by asking God to fill him with love
  (see Ps. 41–42).

After reading the list of what David did, is your desire as deep as you thought? Are you opening your mouth very wide, or are you panting for God's Word very hard? God can give you the desire to have the desire. At one point, when David felt incapable of opening his own mouth, he cried, "O Lord, open my lips" (Ps. 51:15). In other words, he cried, "Give me the desire!"

"Opening our mouths" means to desire God with every fiber of passion in our hearts—and when that desire is absent, to desire the desire we lack. He has promised that when we open our mouths, He will fill them up: "For he satisfies the thirsty and fills the hungry with good things" (Ps. 107:9). The Word is very near—already in us. When we open our mouths, He will do for us what He did for Isaiah.

To close today's lesson, read and prayerfully respond to the invitation that God extends in Isaiah 55:2. Open your mouth with desire, or express your desire to desire. God will surely put His words in your mouth and transform your speech.

128

Saying "I'm sorry."

Apologizing for our mistakes is an important part of building relationships. We ought to be quick to accept responsibility and apologize for our offense, even if the other person's offense is greater.

When we apologize, we should **first** identify what we have done wrong. Is it a critical attitude? A harsh tone of voice? A snap judgment? Impatience? **Second**, an apology should include an admission of guilt: "I was wrong." In admitting guilt, we accept responsibility for our actions. We indicate that our poor behavior was our fault–and not the other person's. **Third**, an apology should include a request for forgiveness. The tone of the apology ought to convey genuine grief that we have injured the other person and violated God's standards. Together, the three parts might look like this: "I shouldn't have yelled at you." (Identify offense.) "I was wrong." (Admit guilt.) "Please forgive me." (Ask forgiveness.)

A Sorry "Sorry"

Some apologies are not apologies at all. Whenever an apology evades responsibility or lays blame elsewhere, it is a sorry sorry. Counterfeit apologies fall into one of three types: Deny, Excuse, or Attack.

Deny that an offense occurred: "I'm sorry, I didn't mean it that way," "I'm sorry you took it that way," and "I'm sorry you felt that way." This type of apology implies that the other person misunderstood our intent. The only mistake was their interpretation.
Excuse the behavior: "I'm sorry, but ..." The message this type of apology conveys is "It wasn't my fault. I couldn't help it."
Attack the other person: "I'm sorry, but you ..." The message is "You made me do it. Your greater offense justifies my lesser offense. You deserved it!" Counterfeit apologies do little to resolve conflict because they send mixed messages. We say we are "sorry," but the rest of our message contradicts that claim.

Ace Your Appreciation

Here's a simple way to ACE your appreciation for someone:

Action: Identify a praiseworthy behavior–verbal, vocal, or visual. (The more specific you can be, the better.)
Character: Identify the character trait the action exemplifies.
Effects: Describe how this action has benefited or blessed you.

For example: "Randy, you devote every Friday night to leading the youth group (action). I appreciate your commitment and tenacity (character). You are providing a good role model for my children (effects)." Or, "Sandra, this brochure looks fabulous! I love what you did with the colors (action). You are so creative (character)! I am proud to hand out a brochure that you have designed (effect)."
Everyone wants to be appreciated. Expressing appreciation is one of the best ways to encourage others. (By the way, the ACE formula is also a great idea for writing thank-you notes.)

Day Four

A Teachable Spirit
The discipline of an instructed tongue

"Those whom I love I rebuke and discipline. So be earnest, and repent."
Revelation 3:19

A few years ago, my youngest son habitually played a Beethoven song with the same wrong note. Advising him of the mistake had not helped, so one day I sat down at the piano with him to correct his error. I pointed to the note on the sheet of music. "This is the note you are playing wrong, Jonathan. What note is this?"

"B," he replied.

"That's right. And what note are you playing?"

He quickly found the note. "A," he concluded.

"So," I said triumphantly, "you are playing the wrong note."

"No I'm not!" he denied. "Beethoven wrote it wrong!"

I couldn't believe it! Even when his error was apparent, he stubbornly refused to be corrected. Sadly, many of us do not outgrow this childish tendency. We arrogantly defy correction. We are angered when others point out our shortcomings or try to correct us.

Disciples Welcome Discipline

I have a friend whose daughter raised a pet sheep. The sheep learned her daughter's voice and would not respond to a command from anyone else. My friend would stand on her back porch and call the sheep at the top of her lungs. No response. Her daughter would come to the steps and call softly. The sheep would appear from nowhere!

Jesus said that His sheep would recognize His voice and follow Him (John 10:27). The most loving thing a shepherd can do is to teach sheep to follow. Following the shepherd is in the best interest of the sheep. Sheep, in turn, must have a teachable spirit.

According to 2 Timothy 3:16, what is Scripture useful for?

1. _____

2. _____

3. _____

4. _____

Discipline is a necessary part of learning how to follow Christ. To learn more about discipline read today's Word from the Word.

[discipline] The Training of a Disciple

Disciple literally means a learner—one who follows both the teacher and the teaching. The Bible refers to disciples of John (see Matt. 9:14); the Pharisees (see Matt. 22:16); Moses (see John 9:28); and Jesus (see Matt. 10:1; Luke 22:11). According to Luke, the members of the early church were known as disciples (see Acts 6:1).

The dictionary defines *discipline* as correction and training. The Greek word, *paideia*, refers to the type of instruction, correction, chastening, and nurture that is involved in training a child. In love, our Heavenly Father disciplines His children (see Heb. 12:6).

The two concepts are inseparably linked. Godly discipline produces better disciples. Christ's disciples are eager to learn and are thus eager to be disciplined. They welcome any instruction, rebuke, or correction that helps them follow Jesus' teachings more closely.

Discipline is not a popular notion. But every parent knows that a lack of discipline results in wayward, unruly children. Read Hebrews 12:5-13. In verse 5, how did the writer regard the topic of discipline, rebuke, punishment, and training?

❏ as something to protest ❏ as a heavy, depressing topic
❏ as an encouraging topic ❏ as something to be outlawed

"My son, do not make light of the Lord's discipline, and do not lose heart when he rebukes you."
Hebrews 12:5

According to verse 7, what does discipline involve?_____

In addition to hardship, discipline also involves pain. Why should we regard the Lord's discipline as a positive, encouraging thing? God uses hardship and pain to train us. He "disciplines us for our good, that we may share in his holiness" (v. 10), and to produce "a harvest of righteousness and peace" in our lives (v. 11). God's discipline is ultimately a sign of His commitment and love.

"Endure hardship as discipline."
Hebrews 12:7

The writer of Hebrews encouraged us not to shrug off (make light of) God's discipline and not to lose heart when we are disciplined. Elsewhere, we are advised not to despise His discipline or resent His rebuke (see Prov. 3:11-12). Disciples welcome discipline. They are teachable. They love to be corrected. They know that the person whom God corrects is "blessed" (Job 5:17; see also Ps. 39:11).

Mockers Reject Discipline

The opposite of a disciple (follower) is a "mocker." Mockers do "not listen to rebuke" (Prov. 13:1). They "scorn instruction" (Prov. 13:13), resent correction, and spurn discipline (see Prov. 15:5). To

During a long life I have had to eat my own words many times, and I have found it a very nourishing diet.
—Winston Churchill

"The proud and arrogant man— "Mocker" is his name; he behaves with overweening pride."
Proverbs 21:24

mock is to ridicule, treat with scorn, defy, scoff, and deride. Mockers do not feel that they need correction and arrogantly resent anyone trying to correct them. They scoff when they are told their words or behavior need correction.

Fill in the following chart comparing the characteristics of mockers and disciples:

Characteristics of a Mocker (Psalm 12:3-4; Zephaniah 3:2)	Characteristics of a Disciple (Jeremiah 10:23-24; 31:18-19)

How God Disciplines

How does the Lord discipline us? We have already seen that He disciplines us through Scripture (see 2 Tim. 3:16). A second way is through the instruction, encouragement, correction, and rebuke of those who are in leadership: church leaders (see 2 Tim. 4:2); parents (see Prov. 13:1); bosses and employers (see Eph. 6:5-9); governing authorities and all other authorities (see Rom. 13:1-5). A third way the Lord might discipline us is through the rebuke of peers and friends (see Prov. 15:12; 25:12; 28:23). Sometimes the words of rebuke may even come from the mouths of enemies (see Gen. 12:18-19).

A final way the Lord can discipline us is through difficult circumstances or difficult people. In Psalm 119, we see that David was disciplined when people slandered, taunted, mocked, lied about, and wronged him without cause.

Read Psalm 119:66-71. In verse 71, what did David conclude?

_____

Later, David said to the Lord, "I know, O Lord, that ... in faithfulness you have afflicted me" (v. 75). David regarded difficult circumstances as discipline from the hand of the Lord—a mark of God's faithfulness. Godly discipline moves us toward the heart of God.

When it comes to your speech habits, do you humbly welcome correction, or do you arrogantly resent it? To harness the power of

132

instruction, we must humbly welcome correction in our speech. Close today's lesson by asking the Lord to give you a teachable spirit. If you have resisted and despised discipline or resented rebuke, confess this sin to Him.

"It was good for me to be afflicted so that I might learn your decrees."
Psalm 119:71

Write your prayer in the space provided.

_____

_____

_____

_____

_____

_____

Constructive Feedback

Some people eagerly correct the faults of others. Other people fear doing so. They know that pointing out areas for improvement risks being misunderstood or rejected. Despite the challenges, constructive feedback is a valuable tool that God encourages us to use wisely for the purpose of building up others.

When giving constructive feedback, precisely define what part of the other person's behavior concerns you. If the concern is based on differences, then you have much less of a right to give feedback than if the concern is about God's standards or for the person's well being. The more precise you can be, the more helpful your feedback will be. Once you have pinpointed your concern, identify some alternatives for what the person could do differently. Carefully consider lines of authority when it comes to "correcting" authority figures. Pray for the right words, the right heart attitude, and the right timing. Follow up your relationship "withdrawal" with a "deposit." Reassure the person that you care about him or her and are committed to the relationship.

Our motivation in giving feedback ought to be for the good of other people–to build them up. Our desire should come out of a genuine interest and affection for them. Far too many people "correct" others out of spite or dislike. Practice humility.

If you are on the receiving end of feedback, receive the feedback graciously and consider it carefully. Even if the bulk of the message is "off base," it just may contain a kernel of truth. Giving and receiving constructive feedback can be a challenge, but the rewards of a message properly given and properly received are enormous.

Day Five

Highest Honors
The triumph of an instructed tongue

"Yet it was good of you to share in my troubles." Philippians 4:14

There's nothing quite as sweet as crossing the finish line in victory. Recently–beating out fierce competition–my son's relay team won a gold medal at a local track meet. Parents snapped pictures. Reporters scribbled on pads. Schoolmates squealed and shouted in jubilation. Honors were awarded.

During the days that followed, Jonathan proudly wore his gold medal everywhere. He showed it to his hockey team, his Sunday school class, his school friends, his neighborhood friends, his grandparents, and even the grocery store clerk–anyone who would listen heard the story of the great track triumph.

Today we approach the finish line for this study. As you complete the last of your daily lessons, I hope you can taste the sweetness of victory in your mouth. I hope that taste will inspire you to keep running toward the goal of speech transformation for the rest of your life.

God's Guarantee

This week we have learned that in order to harness the power of instruction, we must continue to push for perfection in our speech. We must become lifelong apprentices of the Master Teacher. We must open our mouths wide with desire for Him to fill us. We must respond to His correction. If we do these things, we will receive highest honors. We will most certainly triumph.

Mockers boast, "'We will triumph with our tongues; we own our lips–who is our master?'" (Ps. 12:4). But disciples know that triumph comes when we recognize that we do not own our lips and we must depend on a different Master.

Read Exodus 4:10-12. What was Moses worried about?
❑ his lack of education   ❑ his poor posture
❑ his inability to speak well   ❑ his crooked nose

Instead of giving him a "you can do it!" pep talk, God rebuked him for his faulty perspective. In verse 11 God reminded Moses of something. What was it?

_____

God made Moses' mouth–and God owned it. Therefore, Moses could trust God to fill it with the right words.

134

God promised Moses that He would help him speak and teach him what to say. God has given you the same guarantee. As we saw in this week's Talk Show, He has made a "covenant" with you. It is as though He has signed a legal obligation or guarantee. What is His guarantee?

Read Isaiah 59:21. Underline God's guarantee.

God's contract with us–His guarantee–is that His Spirit is with us, and that He will put His words in our mouths–"from this time on and forever"!

Personalize His guarantee by writing your name in the blanks:

"My Spirit, who is on _____, and my words

that I have put in _____ mouth will not depart

from _____ mouth!"

Signed,
Father God, the Almighty

"'As for me, this is my covenant with them,' says the Lord. 'My Spirit, who is on you, and my words that I have put in your mouth will not depart from your mouth, or from the mouths of your children, or from the mouths of their descendants from this time on and forever,' says the Lord." Isaiah 59:21

God put words in Moses' mouth. He put words in Isaiah's mouth (see Isa. 51:16). He put words in Ezekiel's mouth (see Ezek. 3:27). And He has put words in your mouth (see Isa. 59:21). To experience the power of transformed speech, you need only to speak what He has already–by His Spirit–put in you to say.

Depending on the Spirit

Even in the most difficult situations, you need not worry about how you will respond, because if you listen, "the Holy Spirit will teach you at that time what you should say" (Luke 12:12). For "from the Lord comes the reply of the tongue" (Prov. 16:1).

What kind of words has God put in your mouth? Check those that are characteristic of you. Underline those you are willing to cultivate with the Spirit's help.
Words that are:

❑ true (week 3, day 1)
❑ gracious (week 3, day 3)
❑ excellent (week 3, day 5)
❑ humble (week 4, day 2
❑ patient (week 4, day 4)
❑ nourishing (week 5, day 5)
❑ honest and open (week 5, day 3)
❑ appropriate (week 5, day 5)

❑ generous (week 3, day 2)
❑ thankful (week 3, day 4)
❑ peaceful (week 4, day 1)
❑ gentle and understanding (week 4, day 4)
❑ self-sacrificial (week 4, day 5)
❑ faithful (week 5, day 2)
❑ tenderhearted (week 5, day 4)

God's Word "sustains the weary" (Isa. 50:4). They are pleasant and sweet; they bring healing (see Prov. 16:24). They give good counsel (see Prov. 27:9). Above all, they praise Him, honor Him, and confess His name (see Ps. 51:14-15; Rom. 10:9-10). God gives the words. We just need to choose to speak them.

Read Ezekiel 37:1-10. In the space below describe what happened when Ezekiel spoke God's words. (See verse 10.)

_____

_____

Transformed speech is powerful. When Ezekiel spoke, the dead, dry bones came to life before his very eyes. Instead of a dismembered wasteland, a vast crowd of living, breathing humans stood to their feet–strong, healthy, and vibrant.

When you speak what God wants you to speak, your words will have the same effect. Broken, dismembered bones will be healed and realigned. Dead, dry skeletons will be clothed with flesh. You will breathe life and hope back into people's spirits. Your friends and loved ones will stand to their feet–reconciled to you and reconciled to God. Just imagine it!

> Thou hast touched me and I have been translated into thy peace.
> —Augustine

"The mouth of the righteous is a fountain of life" (Prov. 10:11). It brings "healing to the bones" (Prov. 16:24). Don't think that what happened with Ezekiel is too hard for you or out of your reach. The Word is very near. It is in your heart that you may obey it and in your mouth that you may speak it (see Deut. 30:11-14).

Go ... and Speak

Recall Exodus 4:12. After reminding Moses who really owned his mouth, God commanded Moses to "go." The same thing happened with Isaiah. The Lord touched his lips with a burning coal from the altar and purified his mouth. Then the Lord asked, "Who will go?"

In eagerness, the one who had previously bemoaned the unclean state of his lips cried out: "Here I am. Send me."

And God said, "Go..." (Isa. 6:5-9).

Ezekiel, too, after eating the sweet words of God was commanded, "go now ... and speak my words to them" (Ezek. 3:4).

Who made your mouth? Is it not God? What has purified your lips? Is it not the sacrifice of His only Son? And what has filled your mouth? Has He not filled it with His own Word?

All that remains, then, is for you to go and speak. He will help you. He will teach you. His Holy Spirit–whose mighty power raised Christ from the dead–is in you. He has promised, "My Spirit, who is on you, and my words that I have put in your mouth will not depart from your mouth" (Isa. 59:21). "I have put my words in your mouth and covered you with the shadow of my hand" (Isa. 51:16).

Go and speak. His power will transform your speech and bring you more and more conversation peace! Run hard! The gold medal is already yours.

Get Connected

The Tongue Tonics contained in this workbook outline practical skills for effective communication. However, the power for transformed speech does not lie in these techniques. How we interact with the people in our lives has more to do with the condition of our spirits than the structure of our words. What is needed, more than techniques, is spiritual power. This power is only available from one source—God. In order to experience transformed speech, we need to connect with Him. Have you ever made that connection? Do you feel as though you are connected now? Without a power source, your efforts at communication will likely short-circuit. Read again the information on page 48 about "Beginning a Relationship with Jesus."

Being connected involves a lifelong commitment to pursue a relationship with God the Father through Jesus Christ in the power of the Holy Spirit. It means that we commit to improving our relationship with God on an ongoing basis—day by day. If you have not yet done so, will you make that commitment now? If you have "pulled the plug" on your relationship with God, will you make the decision to reconnect? Tell someone you trust about your decision. Get connected and stay connected to the source of the power of transformed speech.

Stay Committed

A fitness consultant once told me that it takes 21 days of consistency to replace an old habit with a new one. Over the years, patterns of behavior and speech habits become deeply ingrained. To overcome negative patterns, intentional, consistent effort is required. Just as in weight training, the results may not be evident immediately, but over time, as you stay with the program, you will begin to notice the difference. Work at putting your new skills into practice. Stay committed. Stay connected to God. His power will transform your speech and bring you more *Conversation Peace.*

The Power of Return
Our words will reap a spiritual harvest.

Week Seven

Harvest is the focal point of every farmer's year. If he has labored well, then he will be rewarded. The power of return–the focus for the final Talk Show, and the seventh and final element for transformed speech–brings us full circle. It is the certainty of harvesting the fruit of our lips that motivates us to continue to work hard at improving our communication skills.

The Bible teaches that we will reap what we sow. It encourages us not to become weary in speaking and behaving well, for at the proper time we will reap a bountiful harvest (see Gal. 6:7-9). As we begin to reap the rewards of improved speech, we look toward the next harvest season. The circle does not end. It continues.
- With the Power of Navigation, we accept responsibility for our speech.
- With the Power of Cause and Effect, we examine our hearts.
- With the Power of Exchange, we establish new patterns.
- With the Power of the Open Gate, we drop our defenses.
- With the Power of Construction, we build others up.
- With the Power of Instruction, we remain teachable.
- With the Power of Return, we enjoy the reward and accept responsibility once again.

In our final Talk Show, we'll see how the process of speech transformation is like the process of growing and harvesting cranberries. At harvest time, cranberry growers flood their fields. Tiny air pockets in the cranberries cause them to float to the surface so they can be harvested. Just imagine the floodwaters of the Holy Spirit gushing over the field of our lives and a bountiful harvest of transformed speech rising up out of our mouths!

The Delaware Indians in New Jersey used the cranberry as a symbol of peace. Labor well with an eye to the harvest–let the power of God transform your speech from the inside out–and you will experience an abundance of conversation peace!

"From the fruit of his mouth a man's stomach is filled; with the harvest from his lips he is satisfied" (Prov. 18:20).

The Power of Return:
Be satisfied with the harvest.
Proverbs 18:20

This diagram will help you follow the video for Session Seven.

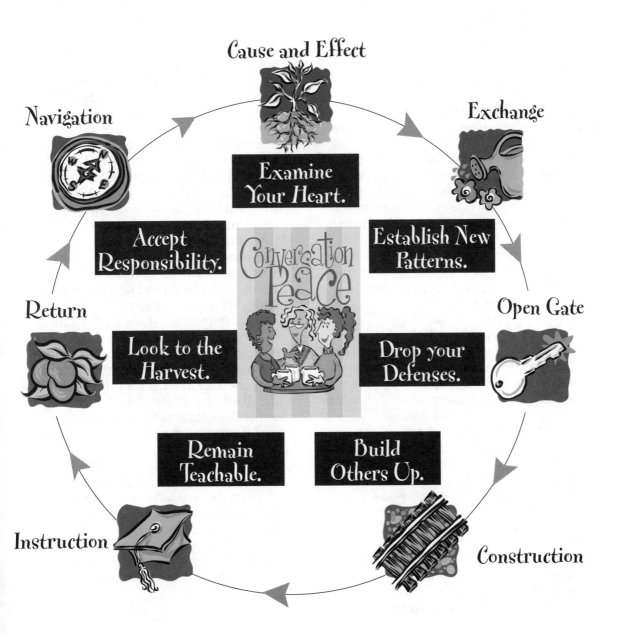

Cause and Effect

Navigation

Exchange

Examine Your Heart.

Accept Responsibility.

Establish New Patterns.

Conversation Peace

Return

Open Gate

Look to the Harvest.

Drop your Defenses.

Remain Teachable.

Build Others Up.

Instruction

Construction

Leader Guide

This leader guide will help you facilitate seven one-hour group sessions. Feel free to adapt these suggestions to fit the needs of your group and the length of your sessions.

Before each session, arrange for a TV and DVD player in your meeting room. Have on hand an attendance sheet, extra Bibles, pens or pencils, and member books. For the first couple of sessions, supply name tags.

Consider enlisting an assistant leader to be responsible for reviewing and providing skills practice for each week's Tongue Tonics. Suggestions are provided on page 145.

This study will interest women of all ages and lifestyles. Begin your publicity at least six weeks in advance of the first meeting. This study does not require an introductory session. Distribute member books in session 1.

Preview each video in order to complete your Talk Show viewer guide before the session. Spend time praying for the study and participants.

Session One

1. As participants arrive, direct them to sign the attendance sheet, prepare a name tag, and pick up a copy of the member book, *Conversation Peace: The Power of Transformed Speech.*
2. Introduce yourself and ask members to do the same. Then ask them to share what they find appealing about this study and what needs they hope will be addressed. List responses on tear sheets or a markerboard.
3. Ask the group to turn to the Table of Contents (p. 3). Review the seven elements of the study. Select volunteers to read aloud "About Mary" and "About This Study" (pp. 4-5).
4. Invite participants to turn through the pages of week 1 as you point to and explain the icons (pictures) representing each part of the week's study: daily lessons, Quips and Quotes, Word from the Word, and Tongue Tonics.
5. Explain the value of completing the learning activities (in bold print) to reinforce what they learn through the content. Since many of these activities involve reading Scripture passages in their own Bibles, affirm that they will be studying God's Word as they learn.
6. Ask a volunteer to read the Breath Freshener (memory verse) for week 1 at the bottom of page 6. Ask participants to turn to page 147. Invite them to cut out each week's Breath Freshener and post it in a location they will see each day or carry it with them in a purse or pocket.

    Encourage them to read this verse frequently during the week, write key words or phrases, and say it to a family member or friend until they can repeat it from memory.
7. Ask participants to turn to the Talk Show guide for week 1 on page 7. Suggest that they take notes and fill in the blanks as Mary Kassian teaches.
8. Play the session 1 DVD (20 min.). Lead the group to review the Talk Show guide, asking appropriate questions and providing answers to the fill-in-the-blank sentences.
9. Assign week 1 in the member book for discussion at the next group session.
10. If members are paying for their books, collect money or explain the procedure for collecting money.
11. Close by praying for openness to God as He reveals ways members can demonstrate transformed speech.

Session Two

1. Ask members to sign the attendance sheet and wear a name tag (optional). Provide member books, pencils or pens, and Bibles as needed.
2. Say together this week's Breath Freshener, 1 Peter 3:10-11. Ask: *How does this passage instruct us to steer our vessels in the right direction?*
3. Review the week 1 Viewer Guide by asking someone to explain the power of navigation. Ask: *How is a tongue like a rudder or a horse's bit?*
4. Review the week 1 daily lessons and guide discussion by leading group members to answer these questions or follow these instructions:
   Day 1: What was your response to the chart on page 8? on page 10? What is your reaction to the Emily Dickinson quote on page 11?
   Day 2: Display your picture on page 12. React to the Washington Irving quote on page 14. Silently react to the question, Will you use your tongue as a sword or a plow? (p. 15) Then pray silently for your commitment to *Conversation Peace.*
   Day 3: What was your response to the map activity on page 17? What are some various ways *word* is used in the Bible? From James 1:5, what are the sources and types of heavenly and counterfeit wisdom?
   Day 4: What was your response to the learning activities on pages 20-22? How do God's rules actually bring us freedom? (p. 21) What does emphasis on the letter *I* do to the pronunciation of *communication*? (p. 22)
   Day 5: Name each of the daily lesson titles as a review of the five aspects of navigation. Did you complete the self-assessment activity on pages 24-26?
5. Review the week 1 Tongue Tonics, or introduce your assistant to lead in this activity. (See p. 145.)
6. Play the session 2 DVD (20 min.). Review responses to the Talk Show guide on page 29.
7. Assign week 2 for the next group session. Close with prayer. Ask God to empower your tongues to better navigate your speech.

Session Three

1. Begin with a check-in time to review members' progress on completing daily lessons. Encourage them to keep up with their reading and learning activities.
2. Say together this week's Breath Freshener, Psalm 19:14. Ask: *Why are the psalmist's names for God appropriate when we talk about godly speech?*
3. From the week 2 Viewer Guide, ask: *What are the two types of soil our words grow in? In your own words, what is the power of cause and effect?*
4. Review the week 2 daily lessons and guide discussion by leading group members to answer these questions or follow these instructions:
   Day 1: Explain your picture on page 31. What is the meaning of *good* from Word from the Word? (p. 32) How do we store up good in our hearts?
   Day 2: What was the meaning of "clean" and "unclean" to the Jews of Jesus' day? Why wasn't Jesus pleased by the Pharisees' standards? (p. 35) Read Matthew 25:26 and explain Jesus' meaning. (p. 36)
   Day 3: Explain how you filled in the blanks on page 38. How did you complete the learning activities on page 39? the chart on page 40?
   Day 4: How did you complete the learning activities on page 42 and the top of page 43? Based on Psalm 51:6, answer the question at the top of page 44. From Word from the Word, explain what you learned about the Devil and

his activities? (p. 44)

Day 5: Share what you drew in the boxes on page 46. What is the relationship between confessing our sins and purifying our speech? (p. 48)

5. Review "Beginning a Relationship with Jesus" on page 48. Explain that you will be available after the session to talk with anyone who prayed to receive Christ.

6. Review the content of the week 2 Tongue Tonics, or call on your assistant to do so (p. 145).

7. Play the session 3 DVD (22 min.). Review responses to the Talk Show guide on page 51.

8. Assign week 3 for the next group session. Close with prayer for the group that your speech will be transformed from the ground of your hearts.

Session Four

1. On a tear sheet or marker board, draw a vertical line and label the left column "Words I will put off" and the right column "Words I will put on." Place several markers on the floor below the chart. As members sign in, ask them to write responses on the chart.

2. Say together this week's Breath Freshener, Ephesians 4:22-24. Read the responses listed on the chart as a confirmation of this Scripture.

3. From the week 3 Viewer Guide review the four ways David adjusted to harness the power of exchange. Select a volunteer to explain in her own words the power of exchange.

4. Review the week 3 daily lessons, and guide discussion by leading group members to answer these questions or follow these instructions:

Day 1: Share with the group some of the lies you struggle with. What is the best way to buckle truth in place? (reading and memorizing Scripture)

Day 2: What are the effects of a focus on scarcity? on abundance? React to this statement: *Our ability to give good to others springs from the abundance of good we receive from God.* Explain how the parable in Matthew 18:21-35 illustrates our relationship with God.

Day 3: From Word from the Word, what is the meaning of *grace*? Illustrate the grace of God by sharing a personal experience. Describe a "grace-giver" (p. 63). How does grace affect our conduct? our speech?

Day 4: From Word from the Word, explain the meaning of *thanks*. Explain "a sacrifice of praise." What is the only reliable source of gratitude? (God)

Day 5: What is the P-48 test? Can you repeat it from memory? How did you complete the chart on page 70?

5. Review the content of the week 3 Tongue Tonics, or call on your assistant to do so. (See p. 145.)

6. Play the session 4 DVD (22 min.). Review responses to the Talk Show guide on page 73.

7. Assign week 4 for the next group session. Close with prayer that members will fill the empty spaces of their hearts with goodness.

Session Five

1. Assign members as pairs or threesomes to review the key points of weeks 1-3. Suggest that they refer to the overview page of each lesson. Allow five minutes for discussion.

2. Say together this week's Breath Freshener, Proverbs 17:19. Ask: *What is a high gate? Why does it bring destruction?*

3. From the week 4 Viewer Guide ask: *What are some causes of Tongue Towers? What are some consequences?* Select a volunteer to explain the power of the open gate.

4. List the names of the gates on a tear sheet or markerboard as you review the week 4 daily lessons and guide discussion. Lead group members to answer these questions or follow these instructions:

Day 1: Why do we battle? Describe a peacemaker. How do we pursue peace?

Day 2: What are the two ways we tear down the gate of control? (p. 79)

Day 3: How does a lack of understanding show up in communication? Describe the communication of a person with understanding.

Day 4: Name the three signs of haste. From the Word from the Word, describe a person who practices biblical patience.

Day 5: List reasons why Christ is our model of servanthood. Why might we hesitate to follow His example?

5. Say, *Every lesson this week has addressed the two opposing attitudes of pride and humility.* As a group, review the primary characteristics of each as it affects our speech.

6. Review the content of the week 4 Tongue Tonics, or call on your assistant to do so. (See p. 145.)

7. Play the session 5 DVD (21 min.). Review responses to the Talk Show guide on page 95.

8. Assign week 5 for the next group session. Close with prayer that members will unleash the power of the open gate by cultivating humility.

Session Six

Consider the optional session plan which follows step 8 on page 144.

1. On the four walls of the room, display a banner with one each of the following phrases:
   Cross barriers
   Create barriers
   Put up obstacles
   Lay track to connect

   As you call out each pair (first two, second two), ask members to stand under the banner that best describes their patterns of communication.

2. Guide discussion of this question: *How can you experience greater harmony in your relationships by using the power of construction?*

3. Ask several volunteers to repeat this week's Breath Freshener, Ephesians 4:29. Draw a vertical line on a tear sheet or markerboard. Label the left column *unwholesome* and the right column *helpful.* As a group, brainstorm the characteristics of each type of speech. List responses in the appropriate column.

4. From the week 5 Viewer Guide ask: *What was Paul's vision for our speech in Ephesians 4:20–5:4? What are some ways we overcome barriers? What kinds of words lay track to connect with others?*

5. Review the week 5 daily lessons and guide discussion by leading group members to answer these questions or follow these instructions:

Day 1: What are some obstacles to encouragement? What are some ways we can encourage others?

Day 2: Contrast unfaithfulness and faithfulness.

Day 3: Contrast dishonesty with honesty. Explain your picture on page 103.

Day 4: Contrast hard-hearted with tenderhearted. Explain how you filled in your chart on page 109.

Day 5: What are examples of timely and untimely words? Give some examples of "building each other up." React to the Spurgeon quote on page 113. What did you write in the margin of page 114?

6. Review the content of the week 5 Tongue Tonics or call on your assistant to do so. (See p. 145.)

7. Play the session 6 DVD (22 min.). Review responses to the Talk Show guide on page 117.
8. Assign week 6 for the next group session. Close with prayer that members would lay tracks of love.

(Optional Plan for Session 6)
1. Secure five pieces of model railroad track, or draw tracks on five separate pieces of heavy paper. Label each piece of track with one of the following words:
   Nourishment
   Faithfulness
   Honesty
   Tenderheartedness
   Discretion
2. Form five groups or assign five individuals, pairs, or threesomes one each of the pieces of track. Give the following assignment:
   a. Describe this quality.
   b. Explain how this quality affects our speech.
   c. Explain how we cultivate this quality.
3. Allow 5-7 minutes for small-group discussion. Call for group reports.
4. Continue with steps 6-8 of the plan for session 6 (see above).

Session Seven

1. Assign members as pairs or threesomes to review the key points of weeks 4-5. Suggest that they refer to the overview page of each lesson. Allow three minutes for discussion.
2. Say together this week's Breath Freshener, Isaiah 50:4. Ask: *What sustains the weary? Which is more important–listening or talking?*
3. From the week 6 Viewer Guide, ask: *What is God's unique guarantee to students who enroll in His School of Speech Arts?* Select a volunteer to explain how we harness the power of instruction.

4. Review the week 6 daily lessons and guide discusion by leading group members to answer these questions or follow these instructions:
   Day 1: What is God's process by which we are being made perfect?
   Day 2: Why was Jesus the perfect student? the perfect teacher?
   Day 3: React to this statement from page 128: "*Your behavior is the best indicator of your desire for transformed speech.*"
   Day 4: React to this statement from page 131: "*Disciples welcome discipline.*" What do you think is the problem when disciples react negatively to discipline? Why do mockers reject discipline? How does God discipline us?
   Day 5: What is God's guarantee to us? (p. 134)
5. Review the content of the week 6 Tongue Tonics, or call on your assistant to do so. (See p. 145.)
6. Ask a volunteer to read aloud page 138, week 7: The Power of Return, in preparation for the final video.
7. Play the session 7 DVD (21 min.). Review responses to the Talk Show guide on page 139.
8. Lead a prayer that members would commit to the lifelong process of speech transformation.
9. Tell about other discipleship studies that are available at present or planned for the future.
10. Lead an appropriate closure activity such as singing a favorite Scripture song or chorus, saying together one of the study's Breath Fresheners, or giving members an opportunity to express thanks for the study and to one another.

Tongue Tonic Review Activities

Use the following suggestions to review the Tongue Tonics for each week's study. If you have selected a person to lead this portion of the session, refer her to this page for guidance in leading the review.

Indicate how much time you have allotted to this review for each session so that she can choose and plan activities.

Session Two

1. Review the three parts of a message from page 11, giving an example of each.
2. Enlist two members to role play the eight potential problems in communication (p. 15). Prepare a script or outline and practice in advance of the session.
3. Ask: *What is the prime objective of receiving and sending a message?* (p. 19).
4. Ask someone to give an example of an "I" statement and explain how this concept aids communication.

Session Three

1. Enlist five volunteers to give one example each of the five barriers to active listening (p. 33).
2. Review the LISTEN-ing skills on page 37.
3. Review the four motivating concerns on page 41.
4. Ask the group to give examples of how we frame, box, and bias as we categorize others with our presuppositions.

Session Four

1. Enlist a volunteer who will carry on a conversation with you as you demonstrate the techniques of echo and inquire (p. 55).
2. Ask someone to explain the difference between manifest and implicit meaning.

3. Ask: *What is a DART?* (p. 63)
4. Ask: *What do the letters SALUTE stand for?* (p. 71)

Session Five

1. Divide into three groups. Assign the groups one each of the following: the question, the statement, and the forecast.
   Ask groups to discuss what they learned about their tool of the trade. After three minutes, call for group reports.
2. Review "I" Statements from page 23.

Session Six

1. Lead a discussion of conflict resolution tools, including: don't get in a dogfight; break conversation chains; identify the crux of the problem; bypass the bait; and resist manipulation.
2. If time permits, illustrate identifying the crux of the problem by explaining these types of problems about which people disagree:
   a. the particulars–facts and data
   b. the process–how to get the job done
   c. the purpose–what will be accomplished
   d. the principle–differences in beliefs, values, and motivations.
3. Illustrate how this information can be valuable in deciding the crux of a conversation chain.

Session Seven

1. Lead a discussion of the importance of a relationship bank balance.
2. Ask: *How should we say "I'm sorry"? What is a sorry sorry?* (p. 129)
3. Ask: *What are some pointers for giving constructive feedback?*
4. Ask: *How does the power of instruction relate to the use and practice of these Tongue Tonics?* (We have to make the process a lifetime commitment.)

Two Ways to Earn Credit
for Studying LifeWay Christian Resources Material

Christian Growth Study Plan resources are available for course credit for personal growth and church leadership training.

Courses are designed as plans for personal spiritual growth and for training current and future church leaders. To receive credit, complete the book, material, or activity. Respond to the learning activities or attend group sessions, when applicable, and show your work to your pastor, staff member, or church leader. Then go to *www.lifeway.com/CGSP,* or call the toll-free number for instructions for receiving credit and your certificate of completion.

For information about studies in the Christian Growth Study Plan, refer to the current catalog online at the CGSP Web address. This program and certificate are free LifeWay services to you.

CONTACT INFORMATION:
Christian Growth Study Plan
One LifeWay Plaza, MSN 117
Nashville, TN 37234
CGSP info line 1-800-968-5519
www.lifeway.com/CGSP
To order resources 1-800-458-2772

Need a CEU?

Receive Continuing Education Units (CEUs) when you complete group Bible studies by your favorite LifeWay authors.

Some studies are approved by the Association of Christian Schools International (ACSI) for CEU credits. Do you need to renew your Christian school teaching certificate? Gather a group of teachers or neighbors and complete one of the approved studies. Then go to *www.lifeway.com/CEU* to submit a request form or to find a list of ACSI-approved LifeWay studies and conferences. Book studies must be completed in a group setting. Online courses approved for ACSI credit are also noted on the course list. The administrative cost of each CEU certificate is only $10 per course.

CONTACT INFORMATION:
CEU Coordinator
One LifeWay Plaza, MSN 150
Nashville, TN 37234
Info line 1-800-968-5519
www.lifeway.com/CEU

Week 5: "Do not let any unwholesome talk come out of your mouths, but only what is helpful for building others up according to their needs, that it may benefit those who listen." Ephesians 4:29

Week 1: "For 'whoever would love life and see good days must keep his tongue from evil and his lips from deceitful speech. He must turn from evil and do good; he must seek peace and pursue it.'" 1 Peter 3:10-11

Week 6: "The Sovereign Lord has given me an instructed tongue, to know the word that sustains the weary. He wakens me morning by morning, wakens my ear to listen like one being taught." Isaiah 50:4

Week 2: "May the words of my mouth and the meditation of my heart be pleasing in your sight, O Lord, my Rock and my Redeemer." Psalm 19:14

Week 7: "From the fruit of his mouth a man's stomach is filled; with the harvest from his lips he is satisfied." Proverbs 18:20

Week 3: "You were taught, with regard to your former way of life, to put off your old self, which is being corrupted by its deceitful desires; to be made new in the attitude of your minds; and to put on the new self, created to be like God in true righteousness and holiness." Ephesians 4:22-24

Week 4: "He who loves a quarrel loves sin; he who builds a high gate invites destruction." Proverbs 17:19